"In this engaging book, Alex Qui
ledge and skills expert reading
reading and to nurture pupils' c
developing the school reading cu
and timely text, which is packed
will be a valuable asset. In openi
reading in an appealing and conversational manner,
paying particular attention to metacognition, Alex offers
the profession evidence-informed tools to reconsider
reading and six steps to close the reading gap. A book
worth buying."

Teresa Cremin, Professor of Education,
Open University, UK

"The science of reading was never a part of my teacher
training and I'd have loved a book like this. Alex Quigley's
Closing the Reading Gap is everything I hoped it would
be; a wonderfully enlightening follow-up to his brilliant
vocabulary book. For those seeking to understand how
reading works, alongside some of the associated debates,
Alex gives us the in-depth research-informed analysis
we're after. He also delivers the accessibility and range of
practical strategies busy teachers need to support children
to read more fluently and to learn more through reading.
Chapters 3 and 4 capture the key concepts we need to understand the complex processes of decoding and comprehension; it's packed with wisdom and insights. Chapter 7,
outlining an array of practical strategies for schools and
teachers, is a magnificent reference for everyone working
in education. I can see this book having a very significant
impact."

Tom Sherrington, author and education consultant

"When over a quarter of 11-year-old pupils do not reach the expected standard in reading, *Closing the Reading Gap* is a welcome and much needed addition to our understanding of the process and difficulty of reading. This wide-compassing book takes us through the history of reading and identifies some of the barriers for many of our pupils and offers many suggestions that professionals can use to support them in this vital aspect of provision.

It is laden with important insights such as 'we are better off with concentrating on the relatively slow, deliberate process of reading for meaning and to understand the subtle difference between reading speedily and reading with fluency'. And when we ask ourselves the questions posed by Alex, we are likely to get better at this important aspect of our practice: what are the 'Goldilocks books' for year 2 ... year 5 and year 9; how will we mediate their complexity, while keeping an eye on the detail of our pupils' reading development; how often do we assume a text that has been read has been understood?

And what resonated powerfully for me is the idea that it is important that pupils read extended texts if they are to grow more sensitive to text structures. If they are predominantly reading PowerPoint slides with condensed phrases, sentences and images, they will not gain experience in tracking more extended text structures. Paradoxically, by making the curriculum more accessible in the short term, we can make it harder to access curriculum reading in the long term.

An important read for all teachers, across all phases and subjects."

Mary Myatt, education adviser and writer, author of
The Curriculum: Gallimaufry to Coherence

"This book should be a core text for all teachers, whether trainees or experienced professionals, whatever their subject or key-stage specialism. Reading success is essential for young people to access any academic curriculum and this book draws together research and effective practice across all subjects and age groups. But not only does it identify and evaluate the symptoms of reading challenges, it provides practical advice and support to 'close the reading gap'. Exam success is underpinned by effective reading tuition, and this book will help every teacher gain a greater understanding of how to teach reading constructively so that academic achievement is attainable for every pupil."

Alison Wilcox, author of the *Descriptosaurus* series

Closing the Reading Gap

Our pupils' success will be defined by their ability to read fluently and skilfully. But despite universal acceptance of reading's vital importance, the reading gap in our classroom remains and it is linked to an array of factors, such as parental wealth, education and book ownership, as well as classroom practice. To close this gap, we need to ensure that every teacher has the knowledge and skill to teach reading with confidence.

In *Closing the Reading Gap*, Alex Quigley explores the intriguing history and science of reading, synthesising the debates and presenting a wealth of usable evidence about how children develop most efficiently as successful readers. Offering practical strategies for teachers at every phase of their teaching career, as well as tackling issues such as dyslexia and the role of technology, the book helps teachers to be an expert in how pupils 'learn to read' as well as how they 'read to learn' and explores how reading is vital for unlocking a challenging academic curriculum for every student.

With a focus on nurturing pupils' will and skill to read for pleasure and purpose, this essential volume provides practical solutions to help all teachers create a rich reading culture that will enable every student to thrive in school and far beyond the school gates.

Alex Quigley is a former English teacher and school leader, of over 15 years' standing, who now works for the Education Endowment Foundation, supporting teachers to access research evidence. He can be found on Twitter @HuntingEnglish and blogs at www.theconfidentteacher.com. His previous books include *Closing the Vocabulary Gap* and *The Confident Teacher*.

Closing the Reading Gap

Alex Quigley

Routledge
Taylor & Francis Group

LONDON AND NEW YORK

First published 2020
by Routledge
2 Park Square, Milton Park, Abingdon, Oxon OX14 4RN

and by Routledge
52 Vanderbilt Avenue, New York, NY 10017

Routledge is an imprint of the Taylor & Francis Group, an informa business

British Library Cataloguing-in-Publication Data
A catalogue record for this book is available from the British Library

Library of Congress Cataloging-in-Publication Data
A catalog record has been requested for this book

ISBN: 9780367276874 (hbk)
ISBN: 9780367276881 (pbk)
ISBN: 9780429297328 (ebk)

Typeset in Celeste and Optima
by Newgen Publishing UK

Printed and bound in Great Britain by
TJ International Ltd, Padstow, Cornwall

To my beautiful children Freya and Noah,

Reading with you each day – and seeing reading through your fresh eyes – was the inspiration and fuel for writing this book.

Contents

Acknowledgements

My efforts to make the subject of reading accessible for teachers in *Closing the Reading Gap* stand on the shoulders of countless reading researchers whose writing has informed every facet of this book. The list of such researchers and writers is extensive, and I will no doubt be guilty of omission, but just some of the experts whose evidence and ideas I hope do some justice include: Dr Jessie Ricketts, Professor Kate Nation, Professor Dan Willingham, Professor Cynthia Shanahan, Professor Tim Shanahan, Dr Mark Seidenberg, Professor Maggie Snowling, Professor Jane Oakhill, Professor Kate Cain, Doug Lemov, Professor Isabel Beck, Professor Kathy Rastle, Professor David Crystal, Professor Teresa Cremin, Dr Wayne Tennant, Professor Tim Rasinski and many more.

I am also indebted to my colleagues at the Education Endowment Foundation (EEF), whose expertise and support have developed my knowledge and understanding, both directly and indirectly informing my writing. I want to pay particular thanks to my EEF colleague, Pete Henderson, whose feedback and discussions helped draft Chapter 5.

I would like to thank Dr Jessie Ricketts and Professor Kate Nation for kindly taking the time during a very busy period to offer me brilliantly useful feedback on chapters from the draft of the book.

A particular thanks must go to my many supportive teacher colleagues. Their insights, friendship and honest feedback ensures that what I write is grounded in the realities of the classroom and communicated in clear, succinct writing for busy teachers. Also, a big thank you to Sonia Thompson, Simon Cox and Becci Jones, for their great school case studies that prove a privilege to share.

A big thank you to Annamarie Kino, my editor, and the team at Routledge for their ongoing support and trust.

Finally, thanks to my partner, Katy – my unofficial editor – who offers me the vital support required to get through the daunting task of book writing.

Once you learn to read, you will be forever free.
Attributed to Frederick Douglass

Introduction

If you can read this, thank a teacher.
Anonymous

As you begin to read this book – word by word, page by page – with seeming effortlessness, you are in fact enacting one of the greatest inventions, and achievements, in human history.

Take a moment to process that fact, as you sit reading on the settee in your pyjamas, or as you ride the train on the way home from work. Enacting this everyday magic is something that you likely take for granted, given that it is so much part of who we are and what we do. Plucking a book from our bookshelves and reading it can prove a daily, near-automatic act for the majority of adults.

In what amounts to only a mere sliver of our evolutionary history – a paltry few thousand years – we have developed our ability to read. As a result, it has propelled our civilisation into modernity.

And so, now, for a mere 250 milliseconds, you will fixate on each word you read – before sweeping automatically from left to right – then near-instantly processing these inky marks into sounds, then transforming them into a rich web of interconnected meaning. That meaning will be plundered from a vast store of knowledge accrued over a lifetime that you'll unlock with apparent ease.

Indeed, a whole world of knowledge will be stored in an hourglass of black print on the page. It all feels at once near magic and, well, something so ... natural.

Reading can feel like our birthright, with our book-shelves becoming an integral part of who we are, shaping our very sense of identity.

Take a moment now to recall your first memory of reading.

For many of us, ruminating on the word 'reading' can unlock potent memories of reading in the cosy lap of a loved one. For me, it evokes a hazy image of my father reading to me at my bedside. Early reading, whether it is in a parent's lap, on the carpet in the classroom, or a snug reading corner, gently but indelibly imprints upon us the mould from which will cast a lifetime of communication in the world. It is why reading can prove both intensely private and public, part of our daily lives in the world, as well as being part of our intimate inner world.

Beyond powerful personal experiences, reading will prove the master skill of school, unlocking the academic curriculum for our pupils. Though the majority of children will go on to learn to read, it will not prove as 'natural' as we think. Yes – many will read fluently and make rapid reading gains, often regardless of the quality of instruction in the classroom – but this will not be the case for all. For too many children, reading is not a right that they acquire with anything like ease. This reality can crash into our consciousness when our pupils struggle to read in our class, or sit an exam, and are barred from understanding words and concepts that we assume every child will know.

For many children in England, their reading ability is steadily improving,[1] yet there are also critical markers to indicate fundamental reading gaps for our pupils that can cut at the very fabric of our society. For example, only 73% of pupils leaving primary school reached the expected level for reading in 2019.[2] Put simply then, one in four children will not read well in school and likely beyond. This reading gap between primary and secondary school can see many pupils unprepared for the changing demands of academic reading in secondary school and with too little time to catch up.

We also know that children of all backgrounds who were read to regularly by their parents at age 5 perform better in maths, vocabulary and spelling at age 16, compared to those who were not read to at home.[3] A Department of Education poll of 2,685 parents also revealed that only a third (31%) of children are read to at home daily.[4] And so, before a child ever sets foot in our schools, with each library that goes unvisited and each story character that goes unmet, the reading gap is opened. If it grows during schooling there is the threat of damaging consequences for individuals and our society.

Small, daily acts of reading matter. Reading gaps can open quickly and near imperceptibly. Research in the United States by Jessica Logan and colleagues,[5] from Ohio State University, calculated that children who were read to daily (around five children's books) would hear well over a million more words (an estimated 1.4 million more) than their peers who were not read to daily. This isn't everyday talk – this is hearing those rare words from books that offer an extra-special value for early language development. Just contemplate the difference for a child's readiness to learn having had so many more rich conversations and shared reading experiences.

Introduction

These glaring societal issues that relate to reading, along with the gargantuan financial figures that attend illiteracy, can simply feel too big and too abstract to grasp. For me, it is the image of an empty bookshelf that gives me pause for thought. Research by the National Literacy Trust reveals the depressing statistic that 1 in 11 children and young people said that they did not have a book of their own at home, with the figure for disadvantaged children rising to 1 in 8.[6]

Take a moment to visualise that empty bookshelf for one or more of those children.

Reading habitually and seeing reading as a pleasurable, fulfilling and motivating activity matters.[7] Put succinctly, 14-year-olds who read often and independently know 26% more words than those who never read.[8] Consider the consequences of that writ large in our classrooms.

In simple terms, able readers read more independently. The reading rich get richer, the reading poor get poorer. This is unsurprising: when you can do something well, it usually is more enjoyable. Given that children's reading ability determines how much they read,[9] as teachers, if we can improve the teaching of reading, then we are likely to increase our pupils' reading ability and how much they read for pleasure.

Regardless of how many books are on the shelf at home then, we can impact how well our pupils read and how much they go on to read. Even small victories can have a significant impact on the school lives of our pupils.

For every pupil in our care then, we are beholden to fill their school day with the richness of countless books, helping them access a wealth of powerful reading experiences, so that they can be buoyed by the world of imagination and knowledge offered to us by possessing the capability to read successfully.

The reading challenge

The school day is typically crammed full of academic reading: from young children reading about magical journeys at story time to teenagers reading dense textbooks. The habitual act of 'learning to read', and going on to 'read to learn', is an ever-present part of school life, both inside and outside of the classroom. For those pupils who lack reading skill, being confronted with reading failures so frequently is a sure-fire way to diminish their enjoyment of and will to engage in school.

For too many, the academic code of school remains inscrutable. Each time they read, the mental bandwidth they expend can prove draining. By stark contrast, for almost every teacher, and for almost all of our successful pupils, reading is an accessible, fluent act that offers a great deal of pleasure, while simultaneously offering us a vital tool to learn. We can prove so expert at reading ourselves that it can be hard to recognise and address the challenges faced by our novice readers.

Try reading the following sentence:

Every teacher is of course an expert reader, but that does not necessarily mean we are experts in how to teach reading successfully.

Just consider for a moment the mental effort you had to exert to comprehend this mirror sentence. In an instant, it can make us mindful of both how skilled we are at grappling with reading challenges, but also how challenging the act of reading can prove for many of our pupils. For those who don't easily map sounds on to letters, cohere patterns, follow reading conventions and speedily draw upon a vast wealth of background knowledge, reading can be an arduous act.

Introduction

Our brains have developed such a rich knowledge of reading that it doesn't rēɑllʏ ɱɑǁǁer *if* Щ℥ яɛɑð wðrÐ§ with RΛDICΛLLY ƆʲFFℇRℇɲⵏ fonts, or in upper or LOWER ᴄⱥsᴇs, we can still readily comprehend what we read. Even faced with reading words without spaces – which was the norm only a few centuries ago – wecanmakesomesenseof whatwereadandconquersignificantbarrierswithalegionofs killedstrategies.

Cracking the special code of reading mere blots of ink can be too easily assumed by those that possess this knowledge. Indeed, the strategies that we deploy in a millisecond can remain inscrutable for too many pupils in our classrooms.

Every teacher can readily recall the painstaking experiences suffered by pupils who more obviously have significant reading barriers, usually leading to a strong desire to better understand how they can help. And yet, more commonly, it is the daily act of reading in the classroom, undertaken by the majority of our pupils, where small, hidden gaps in knowledge and understanding occur. It can be as minor as tripping over a few words, not grasping a phrase or failing to visualise and really grasp an important scientific process being described in dense, technical vocabulary. Over time these marginal, concealed gaps in reading comprehension aggregate into the very difference between academic success and failure.

Take the following couple of sentences from a national assessment:

> There wasn't the slightest breeze to cool the skin or make even a baby-finger crease on the surface of the sea. The Louisa May floated like a toy sitting on a glass table.
>
> 'An Encounter at Sea',
> 2017 KS2 SATS reading paper

This opening passage from a recent SATs reading exam paper managed to trip up many a 10-year-old. For us, as expert readers, in an instant, we can visualise the scene. We bridge the setting of the sea with the name "Louisa May" as that of a ship. Our word knowledge combines with our grammar knowledge – synchronised deftly with our deep knowledge of stories and their patterns – to make sense of the description. We sweep across the gap between sentences, bridging between "sea" and "the", by drawing upon a world of knowledge and ample reading skill. In truth, *we* do this with consummate ease.

But what about the many pupils who don't take the subtle grammatical cue to infer the name of the ship? Are they further hampered by the poetic style that silkily combines similes and metaphors to evoke the scene? Can they decipher a "baby-finger crease"?

Perhaps they spot the article 'the' and unravel the simile, thereby knitting together these two sentences. Perhaps they don't. It is these small gaps in knowledge and understanding, hidden in plain sight, that accumulate and determine just how well they learn and remember in the classroom.

What makes the following passage from a GCSE religious education textbook a challenge for the vast majority of our teen pupils?

> The third pillar of Islam is Zakah. This means giving alms (giving money to the poor). For Muslims who have enough savings, it is compulsory to give 2.5 per cent of those savings every year to help the poor. Many Muslims will work out how much they owe and give the money at the end of Ramadan.
>
> By giving Zakah, Muslims are acknowledging that everything they own comes from God and belongs to

him, and that they should use their wealth to remember God and give to those in need. It frees people from desire, and teaches self-discipline and honesty.

Zakah literally means to purify or to cleanse. Muslims believe that giving Zakah helps to purify the soul, removing selfishness and greed.

> *GCSE Religious Studies for AQA A: GCSE Islam*,
> by M. Fleming, P. Smith, & D. Worden, p. 40[10]

As an expert adult reader, you'll likely recognise that you are working hard to cohere this passage. Of course, the more background knowledge you have about Islam the better. The more vocabulary knowledge you can draw upon the better, including academic vocabulary, such as "compulsory", "acknowledging" and "self-discipline" – not just the subject-specific terminology of the Islamic faith, such as "Zakah" and "Ramadan".

Alongside this essential background and vocabulary knowledge, some of the seemingly accessible vocabulary, like "this", "for" and "it" actually act as important 'cohesive ties'. That is to say, those crucial words that link together the sentences and ideas. These are crucial transition points that are more meaningful in this passage than they may seem to some of our weaker readers. If the teacher is reading this passage to pupils, simply stressing these words as we read can prove a small, effortless aid to reading comprehension.

More subtly, for the vast majority of teachers who do not have a great deal of knowledge of linguistics, we draw upon our understanding of grammatical conventions – such as the use of parentheses (more commonly described as brackets). The aforementioned words that act as cohesive ties show how sentences are inextricably linked in ways that may appear obvious to a highly skilled reader, but not for our pupils, who usually lack knowledge and practice when it comes to academic reading.

To read this single paragraph about the Islamic faith demands knowledge of the world, of reading, text structures, sentences structures and word knowledge[11] – all to be orchestrated at near-instantaneous speed.

For older pupils reading this textbook in secondary school, such challenging informational texts are the norm. Crucially, however, given that the majority of teachers in English schools are offered little training on how to teach academic reading,[12] many pupils are left to sink or swim. For a teacher who isn't well trained in the science of reading, it can be hard to know if pupils are waving or drowning as they read at their desks.

As pupils progress through school, they experience a gradual increase in reading challenge. It is vital that at each step teachers recognise the fundamental causes of reading barriers faced by pupils, while helping our pupils negotiate the ever-increasing trajectory of challenge in the texts they read, in school and beyond. In international reading tests, English pupils fared worse on informational texts than narrative texts,[13] suggesting that the reading challenge may be particularly acute for pupils in this area of reading. Given the proportion of informational texts increases significantly in secondary school, we should pay close attention to this issue.

From the position of expert readers, it can be too easy to miscalibrate the reading challenge faced by our less-experienced pupils. Whether it is reading about the *Louisa May*, or the Islamic faith, to successfully develop our pupils' knowledge of the world, we need every teacher to carefully attend to our pupils' store of words, while helping pupils to best learn the vital strategic act of 'reading to learn'.

Introduction

The teacher knowledge gap

American psychologist, Professor Lee Shulman, aptly compared the complexity of teaching to the experience of a doctor in an emergency room during a natural disaster.[14] Clearly, Lee was familiar with teaching after lunch on a rainy and wind-swept Thursday afternoon just before the end of term. Now, this description of high complexity in the classroom could equally encompass the difficulty a teacher faces in attempting to understand and teach reading, given the variable reading knowledge, gaps and barriers faced by our pupils.

Unfortunately, despite reading proving the master skill of school, teachers receive too little high-quality training on teaching reading. For well over a century, there have been contentious debates on how to best teach children how to read – labelled appropriately the 'reading wars'.[15] In reality, most teachers have long been deaf to the warring factions and have instead cobbled together what training they can on phonics, fluency, vocabulary instruction, reading comprehension and similar. Many secondary school teachers, typically untrained, do not even fully recognise the scale of the reading demand facing our pupils.

It is unsurprising that teachers are not expert in how children learn to read, the complex processes that underpin reading, nor the barriers faced by our pupils. Specific topics, like dyslexia, prove contentious[16] and much of the guidance is unclear, with some even proving contradictory. What are teachers to believe? And where are teachers going to find the time to absorb the many developments in reading science?

Pushed for time, invariably with too little training and tools devoted to the matter, we are typically weak at updating our understanding and sharing our knowledge of reading – and our young readers – across phases and across our schools.

For teachers in Key Stage 1 (KS1), knowledge of learning to read, structured phonics and developing vocabulary knowledge is a prerequisite, but by early Key Stage 2 (KS2), a different, more nuanced knowledge of the intricacies of reading comprehension and text structures is required. Indeed, the most important processes that attend reading in Key Stage 3 (KS3) prove more similar to that of KS2. And yet, often too little time and thought are given over to the critical academic transition between primary and secondary school.[17] Pastoral matters – moving to 'big school' – are rightly prioritised; however, reading in year 7 – founded on reading dense informational texts for almost all of the school day – marks a significant shift from year 6, where fiction still tends to dominate the daily reading diet.

Secondary school teachers do rightly prioritise the development of subject expertise, but how we read uniquely as a historian, a geographer or a scientist, should actually prove a vital thread in such development. We must remember that for the one in four pupils 'below expected' reading skill in year 7, such development of subject expertise will inevitably be stunted.

Every scientist, by way of example, becomes more proficient and knowledgeable via the medium of academic reading. Helping pupils to strategically read a science textbook requires careful and knowledgeable instruction. Now, a secondary school science teacher likely shouldn't be swamped with training on how children learn to read, given that the majority of their pupils will be beyond that point, but targeted support and training are required on most facets that define the act of reading, given that it mediates the school curriculum.

Introduction

To prove the point, try and find out how many of your teacher colleagues feel confident in supporting a pupil diagnosed with dyslexia, or with poor comprehension in their classroom. The results will likely prove chastening.

Most children do learn to read with success in the first years of school, but reading expertise continues to develop into, and throughout, adolescence. It is therefore imperative that *every* teacher is supported with age-appropriate knowledge of teaching reading. Teachers being good readers themselves will not prove enough.

Now, it is clear that for primary school teachers, the joy of story time on the carpet is powerfully emotive and satisfying. This can be in stark contrast to some of the more technical and difficult aspects of reading skill that can appear mundane and bloodless. And yet – remember – reading isn't as 'natural' as we may assume, and every teacher would benefit from understanding more about the tremendous complexity of reading and how to teach it more effectively.

Teachers possessing gaps in their knowledge about how to teach reading is compounded by teaching in a climate of high-stakes assessment that can actively inhibit reading development. Given we exist with a high-stakes accountability system, along with limited teacher training, we see teachers driven to enact lots of narrow exam practice. SATs preparation can be reduced to lots of reading comprehension practice composed of a legion of small, digestible gobbets of reading texts. Instead of focusing upon our efforts to develop reading comprehension, fluency and building reading stamina, we can over-practise test items that chop up extended texts, so that pupils do not build up the requisite knowledge to actually become *better* readers.

In their exploration of the enacted curriculum in English schools, the Office for Standards in Education, Children's

Services and Skills (Ofsted) have noted that foundation subjects like science, history, technology, etc. have been marginalised in the primary curriculum.[18] Of course, we know that pressures around accountability and SATs examinations can drive such behaviours. Paradoxically, reading researchers have stated that it is the crucial background knowledge offered by these foundational subjects that helps determine our pupils' ability to read complex academic texts throughout the school curriculum.[19] It is reading that determines exam success, along with many more benefits.

In secondary school, equally driven by expediency, teachers invariably distil complex texts on to the narrow, limited boundaries of the PowerPoint slide. Indeed, the language of textbooks has been simplified over time too with academic English being made more accessible.[20] Though PowerPoint presentations may offer useable tools for teaching, if they serve as a primary method to reduce the complexity of what our pupils read, then it will inhibit our pupils undertaking the necessary practice of reading extended, complex texts.

How many pupils will go unprepared to navigate the cavernous aisles of the university library? How many pupils will be barred from the corridors of power altogether because they cannot read broadly and deeply?

The depressing truth is that reading doesn't always receive the primacy in the classroom that it deserves. It can be crowded out by a variety of reasons that we must address, school by school, classroom by classroom. Indeed, in one online questionnaire, teachers reported that in the year 4 classroom only around 15% of teachers read to their class every day.[21] We should ask: Who suffers most from this lack of reading? The answer: It is the pupils who have the empty bookshelves, or just as likely, no bookshelf at all.

Closing the reading gap in the classroom and beyond the school gates

So, what has reading ever done for us?

It profoundly affects our lives, offering us a vehicle to store and share the essential knowledge of our culture. The inextricable links between reading, literacy and health, wealth and well-being are well established. It is not just a means to other ends. It is an end in itself that proves one of the greatest of rewards for living.

For me, reading is essential to my professional life, but also intensely personal. Diving into books opened up doors that were denied to my parents. I was able to go to university to study on the basis of my academic reading. Though my parents weren't able to help me interpret the weighty academic tomes of secondary school or beyond, I look back now and recognise the reading-rich environment they had tacitly created. My mother would be endlessly buried in a story, while my father would survey newspapers – the *Liverpool Echo* and the *Daily Mirror* – each day, cover to cover, and we'd talk through the sports news as a daily ritual.

With my own children, I seize on every available opportunity to cultivate a love of reading and to share books with them. We support them to read daily. If my young daughter becomes inquisitive about science or politics, I'll order a book online and it will be in her hand the next day. Our nightly shared reading helps drive their reading skill,[22] motivating them to read more and enjoy it. Of course, as they gobble up their annual shelf-full of books, their word wealth grows and school success becomes more likely. For my children, reading for pleasure and purpose becomes something of a self-fulfilling prophecy.

Motivation and reading for pleasure begin early for every child – before they even get to school.[23] For those pupils who lack the material and cultural supports beyond the school gates, whose motivation is likely to be dimmed on entry, we need to do everything in our power to support them. We need to quickly cultivate and sustain their reading skill, thereby offering our pupils opportunities to experience success in reading. Supporting skilled early reading will have countless benefits for our pupils as they progress through school.

Research evidence strongly links reading fiction and the reading of newspapers with teenagers' reading skill.[24] Though our teen pupils are usually reading informational texts, the rich, regular exposure to the words, ideas and knowledge enshrined in fiction that still helps support their school success. We can go one better and attend to encouraging the reading of lots of fiction for pleasure, while aiding teachers to train pupils in reading informational texts strategically, so that they can, with seeming effortlessness, read like a historian, a scientist or a geographer, etc.

It is a simple truth: successful reading helps determine academic success. Reading proves the master skill of school.

So what knowledge is a prerequisite for every teacher to teach reading in the most effective way possible? What plans can we put in place to further develop upon our existing efforts?

We can start with the following steps, supported by this book:

1. Train teachers to be expert in how pupils 'learn to read' and go on to 'read to learn'.
2. Develop and teach a coherent and cumulative 'reading rich' curriculum.
3. Teach with a focus on reading access, practice and enhancing reading ability.

4. Teach, model and scaffold pupils' reading so that they become strategic and knowledgeable readers.
5. Nurture pupils' motivation to read with purpose and for pleasure.
6. Foster a reading culture within, and beyond, the school gates.

IN SHORT ...

- The reading gap emerges early, before pupils attend school, typically worsening over time without significant intervention. At points of transition, such as between primary and secondary school, the gap can become more acute and problematic.
- The act of daily reading matters. Young children who are read to daily can hear up to a million more words a year than their peers who are not read to by their parents or caregivers.
- The reading pupils undertake in school is typically more complex than other forms and requires substantial background knowledge and reading skill. Informational texts can prove uniquely challenging for pupils, given they use more specialist and rare vocabulary, and less common text structures, when compared with many fiction texts.
- Though teachers are expected to teach via the medium of academic reading on a daily basis, most teachers have a knowledge gap regarding understanding reading development and how to teach reading in the classroom most effectively.
- Reading proves the master skill of school, so we need to nurture our pupils' reading will and skill.

Notes

1 Mullis, I. V. S., Martin, M. O., Foy, P., & Hooper, M. (2017). *PIRLS 2016 international results in reading.* Retrieved from http://timssandpirls.bc.edu/pirls2016/international-results.

2 Department for Education (2019). *National curriculum assessments at key stage 2 in England, 2019 (interim).* Retrieved from www.gov.uk/government/publications/ national-curriculum-assessments-key-stage-2-2019-interim/ national-curriculum-assessments-at-key-stage-2-in-england-2019-interim.

3 Sullivan, A., & Brown, M. (2013). *Social inequalities in cognitive scores at age 16: The role of reading.* London: Centre of Longitudinal Studies.

4 Department for Education (2018). *The childcare and early years survey of parents 2017.* Retrieved from https://assets. publishing.service.gov.uk/government/uploads/system/ uploads/attachment_data/file/766498/Childcare_and_Early_ Years_Survey_of_Parents_in_England_2018.pdf.

5 Logan, J. A. R., Justice, L. M., Yumuş, M., & Chaparro-Moreno, L. J. (2019). When children are not read to at home: The million-word gap. *Journal of Developmental & Behavioral Pediatrics, 40*(5), 383–386. doi:10.1097/DBP.0000000000000657.

6 Clark, C., & Picton, I. (2018). *Book ownership, literacy engagement and mental wellbeing.* London: National Literacy Trust.

7 Taboada, A., Tonks, S., Wigfield, A., & Guthrie, J. T. (2009). Effects of motivational and cognitive variables on reading comprehension. *Reading & Writing Quarterly, 22,* 85–106; Breadmore, H., Vardy, E. J., Cunningham, A. J., Kwok, R. K. W., & Carroll, J. M. (2019). *Literacy development: A review of the evidence.* Retrieved from https://educationendowmentfoundation. org.uk/public/files/Literacy_Development_Evidence_ Review.pdf.

8 Sullivan, A., Moulton, V., & Fitzsimons, E. (2017). *The intergenerational transmission of vocabulary.* Working paper, Centre for Longitudinal Studies. Retrieved from https:// cls.ucl.ac.uk/wp-content/uploads/2017/11/CLS-WP-201714-The-intergenerational-transmission-of-vocabulary.pdf.

9 Van Bergen, E., Snowling, M. J., de Zeeuw, E. L., van Beijsterveldt, C. E. M., Dolan, C. V., & Boomsma, D. I. (2018). Why do children read more? The influence of reading ability on voluntary reading practices. *Journal of Child Psychology and Psychiatry, 59*(11), 1205–1214.

10 Fleming, M., Smith, P., & Worden, D. (2016). *GCSE religious studies for AQA A: GCSE Islam.* Oxford: Oxford University Press, p. 40.

11 Best, R. M., Floyd, R. G., & Mcnamara, D. S. (2008). Differential competencies contributing to children's comprehension of narrative and expository texts. *Reading Psychology, 29*(2), 137–164. doi:10.1080/02702710801963951.

12 Mullis, I. V. S., Martin, M. O., Foy, P., & Hooper, M. (2017). *PIRLS 2016 international results in reading.* Retrieved from http://timssandpirls.bc.edu/pirls2016/international-results.

13 Ibid.

14 Shulman, L. (2004). *The wisdom of practice: Collected essays of Lee Shulman: Volume 1.* San Francisco, CA: Jossey-Bass.

15 Castles, A., Rastle, K., & Nation, K. (2018). Ending the reading wars: Reading acquisition from novice to expert. *Psychological Science in the Public Interest, 19*(1), 5–51. https://doi.org/10.1177/1529100618772271.

16 Elliott, J. G., & Grigorenko, E. L. (2014). *The dyslexia debate.* New York, NY: Cambridge University Press.

17 Education Endowment Foundation (2019). *Improving secondary literacy.* London: Education Endowment Foundation.

18 Ofsted (2018). *An investigation into how to assess the quality of education through curriculum intent, implementation and impact.* December 2018, No. 180035. Retrieved from https://assets.publishing.service.gov.uk/government/uploads/system/uploads/attachment_data/file/766252/How_to_assess_intent_and_implementation_of_curriculum_191218.pdf?_ga=2.94315933.1884489255.156683899 1-1949876102.1566494836.

19 Willingham, D. (2017). *The reading mind: A cognitive approach to understanding how the mind reads.* San Francisco, CA: Jossey-Bass.

20 Biber, D., & Gray, B. (2016). *Grammatical complexity in academic English.* Cambridge, UK: Cambridge University Press.

21 Teacher Tapp (2018). What teacher tapped this week. No. 60, 19 November. Retrieved from https://teachertapp.co.uk/what-teacher-tapped-this-week-60-19th-november-2018.

22 Dickinson, D. K., Griffith, J. A., Golinkoff, R. M., & Hirsh-Pasek, K. (2012). How reading books fosters language development around the world. *Child Development Research, 2012*. http://dx.doi.org/10.1155/2012/602807.

23 Chapman, J., Tunmer, W., & Prochnow, J. (2000). Early reading-related skills and performance, reading self-concept, and the development of academic self-concept: A longitudinal study. *Journal of Educational Psychology, 92*, 703–708. doi:10.1037/0022-0663.92.4.703.

24 Jerrim, J., & Moss, J. (2019). The link between fiction and teenagers' reading skills: International evidence from the OECD PISA Study. *British Educational Research Journal, 45*(1), 181–200.

2 A history of reading

Those who read see twice as well.

Menander, fourth century BC

Picture a familiar scene. A class of pupils head into their classroom, chattering away about their latest break-time game. Quickly, they are hushed by their teacher and so they sit obediently, ready to get writing on their tablets.

Only these tablets are made of clay ... and this classroom scene is around 5,000 years ago – in Sumer, Mesopotamia (now better known as southern Iraq).

In all this time, we have moved from reading on small clay tablets to ... well, shiny electronic tablets.

Sumerian pupils took years to learn their language in their 'tablet house' schools. In remarkably traditional fashion, still reminiscent of teaching today, teachers would write and mould the symbols on one side of the small clay tablet, before pupils then wrote the memorised symbols on the reverse side of the tablet. It was, effectively, an ancient version of 'look – cover – write – check'.

These early Mesopotamian tablets were effectively pocketsize – around three inches across – very like our modern smartphones. A pouch of these tablets would form the rudimentary first 'books'.

Though it is the memorable pictograms (a picture-based system for symbolising words or phrases) best represented by Egyptian hieroglyphs that have most famously endured, it is in Sumer – with their cuneiform writing – where we find the origins of our written language system. The birth of reading begins here. The word 'cuneiform' comes from the Latin meaning 'nail' – deriving from the visual appearance (tantamount to imprints of crows' feet) resulting from the pointed reed pen used to mark on the soft clay tablets.

Try a little cuneiform reading for yourself. Trace the cuneiform 'letters' in Figure 2.1.

Now, read on a little – perhaps take a break or grab a cup of coffee – then try to write down some of these 'letters' from your visual memory with the book closed. Return back to the cuneiform in Figure 2.1 after you have committed your efforts to paper.

How did you do? Could you memorise these rudimentary letters?

It no doubt proves tricky to burden our memory with a feat of visualising and remembering these complex early symbols and languages. It makes clear why we developed our brilliantly efficient alphabet that attached common letters to a range of sounds. Learning the thousands of signs of cuneiform would take well over six years of laborious

He   el   pe

Figure 2.1   Mesopotamian cuneiform

effort. And yet, if you take a group of young pupils to the British Library, they can have great fun scratching away at imitating and translating this early script in quick time (see Figure 2.2).

Figure 2.2   Cuneiform clay tablet: summary account of silver for the governor written in Sumerian Cuneiform on a clay tablet. From Shuruppak or Abu Salabikh, Iraq, *c.*2500 BCE, British Museum, London. BM 15826

Source: Author Gavin Collins, 2010. Retrieved from http://commons. wikimedia.org/wiki/File:Sumerian_account_of_silver_for_the_ govenor.JPG.

Many of the exact truths of Sumerian culture and the birth of reading, akin to the life of Shakespeare, are an incomplete history shrouded by some mystery. And yet, we can be confident that the human voice was first committed to print in ancient societies largely to ensure transactions and contracts were, quite literally, set in stone (and clay).

Reading as a personal pleasure likely came much later than this Sumerian society. Reading was instead primarily part of the business of life and work, such as recording sales of livestock. It was almost exclusively boys who would have been taught to read, though some girls from royal houses learnt to read. Perhaps around 1 in 100 would have learnt to read in ancient Sumerian and Egyptian cultures, thereby conferring power and status on to everyone who could do so, from scribing slaves to kings.

An enduring Mesopotamian maxim stated: "Let the tutored instruct the tutored, for the untutored may not see."

From soft, clay tablet to shining new technological tablet, there is an instructive continuity in how we read, as well as significant changes that every teacher can observe and learn from. Indeed, if we better learn the history of the story of reading, we will learn a great deal about how we read now, while envisioning some predictions about how we should do so in the future. In short, we all need to be tutored in the memorable history of reading.

If you know your history …

Why don't we teach every primary-school-age child one of the greatest stories ever told: the story of how we learnt to read?

Though we know that there are cave drawings, such as the Lascaux caves in France, dating back to Palaeolithic humans, from around 16000 BCE, the first known 'book' – the 'Pruss Papyrus' (from c.2500–2350 BCE) – is far more recent. In what is an incredibly short time, given the span of human history, we have seen the remarkable act of reading transform how we live. Not only that, reading also offers not only the crucial vehicle for progress, it is also the record of the self-same progress that is passed on from generation to generation.

We have only been reading as a species for less than 5,000 years. As such, our brains have not yet developed a neural architecture especially designed for reading. Instead, we hijack the brain's auditory systems, based on our crucial hearing of speech, as well as our language system, to translate speech sounds into print. Our ability to read then is not 'natural' like learning to talk or walk. This story of our developing reading brain gives us essential knowledge to better understand how to teach such a vital but difficult act. It will prove more difficult and 'unnatural' than talking and it will require the best classroom instruction that we can muster.

What we read now barely resembles the distant origins of our reading systems. Beginning in classical antiquity, the language systems we read developed from simple notches on sticks and walls – denoting animals sold, or contracts agreed – to pictograms of said animals and much more.

Over many hundreds of years though, people recognised that this system was inefficient and that logograms – a written character that represents a word or a phrase – would prove easier. This was made more efficient still when we devised alphabets that represented sounds as letters, so that you could compose many words with relatively few letters. And so 'owl' would become 'ow', and so on. Then, with a small number of letters, we could represent many more sounds and words (see Figure 2.3). Subsequently, teaching children to read became much more about learning this all-important alphabetic code.

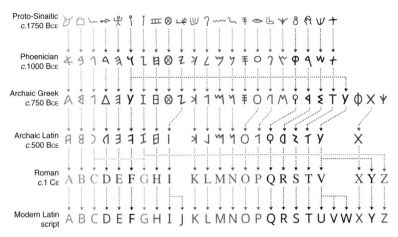

Figure 2.3 Evolution of the alphabet

Source: Author Matt Baker, 2018. Retrieved from https://cdn. shopify.com/s/files/1/1835/6621/files/alphabet-bw_be19cb7a-4aed-4407-9d53-b73230415443.png. Creative Commons BY-SA-NC, UsefulCharts.com.

When we go digging into the famed ancient societies of Greece and the Roman Empire, we recognise the first emerging literate societies. It was reading and writing that spread such empires and advanced every facet of their society.

There were a few sceptics who feared reading 'books'. Socrates, no less, worried that reading would deteriorate our memory for speech. We know he was patently wrong because his words were recorded by his disciple, Plato – in a book – which has preserved it in our collective memory better than any oral tradition possibly could. Conversely, other great figures in history, like Alexander the Great, a pupil of Aristotle, was a lover of reading and made the act of reading prestigious and important. Though reading was still largely circumscribed to only the ruling classes – with only the wealthy owning books – a narrow minority of slaves were trusted to read for their masters.

Over time, reading would fundamentally democratise knowledge, across ancient societies and the known world.

Reading in ancient times was conceived as something to be heard and not the more silent, contemplative act we typically assume today. Given its different purpose, we can recognise that the writing we take for granted now looks significantly different too. In our classical past, writing would be depicted in *'scriptura continua'*.[1] That is to say, there would be no spaces between words, punctuation, nor the other organisational features we assume to constitute 'writing'. This script imitated 'natural' speech in its continuous flow. This made sense given that 'reading' was very much considered an oral act. Given that most people were illiterate, public readings were common.

Reading was to become a more personal and typically silent act over time. Around AD 383, in his 'Confessions', Saint Augustine thought it so odd to see silent reading that he noted down this odd occurrence when observing Saint Ambrose reading: "When he read his eyes scanned the page and his heart sought out the meaning, but his voice was silent and his tongue was still."[2]

Without doubt, reading in silence became much easier to do once writing became clearer to read. Spacing and other helpful organisational features began to emerge in the seventh century – which likely helped drive the significant shift to seeing reading as typically 'silent' and an act that is predominantly undertaken 'in our heads'.[3]

Another feature so important to reading and writing today was punctuation. Again, it is another relatively recent invention. Punctuation is popularly attributed to Aristophanes of Byzantium – in around 200 BC – but was not as organised as we know it now.[4] Around the eighth century onwards, full stops were indicated by dashes and points and paragraphs were demarcated with a larger first letter. We can be sure our year 3 pupils wouldn't get away with such a slapdash approach!

Religious reading has dominated the developing history of reading, while also being intertwined with education and learning to read. The act of reading was synonymous with acts of worship, from reading the Bible, the Quran and the Torah – with Jewish families going on to explicitly celebrate the ritual act of reading. There is a mixed history, whereat religious orders have been integral in teaching reading, while there have been times where the church authorities held a vested interest in it not being available to the masses. Indeed, Algonse de Spina complained that the origin of heresy (those beliefs or opinions contrary to religious faith) could be attributed to the silent, unsupervised reading that Saint Augustine found so strange.[5] He wasn't wholly wrong either – the silent revolution of reading would irrevocably change how we live.

If boys in Sumeria begin a long history that links to the practices of our young pupils today, then it was the religious scholars of the Middle Ages who were taught to read in very specific, laboured ways, which probably best represents the studious act of our older pupils in contemporary classrooms.

Scholars in the Middle Ages would undertake elaborate rereadings. First, the '*lectio*' would see scholars analyse the grammar of what was being read, before undertaking the '*littera*', which was a literal reading of the text. This was followed by the '*sententia*', whereat scholars would read what other accepted commentators discussed about the meaning of the text in question. Of course, rereading and careful close reading is still crucial in the classroom today. Indeed, modern-day reading experts recommend approaches to strategic rereading in the classroom that is founded on similar principles.[6]

When our pupils are caught complaining about being tired from reading and thinking hard, we can point them to scholars from the Middle Ages and their endless hours studying the Bible and making painstaking notes. Labelled 'glosses', these marginal notes are very similar to how we still make marginal notes today. The act of reading in the classroom became privileged. Indeed, in thirteenth-century Spain, King Alfonse el Sabio demanded that teachers must read entire books to their classes unabated – unless they were in considerable ill health![7]

We can see in the education of the Middle Ages how the act of reading in the classroom properly emerges. It is such a part of the fabric of education and what happens in the classroom nowadays that we take it for granted as simply 'natural'. For our novice pupils it likely proves as unnatural and difficult as it did for Sumerian scholars, or monks from the Middle Ages.

In undertaking the act of strategic, careful close reading of academic texts, reading, taking notes, rereading and eking out new layers of meaning, our pupils begin to closely resemble their Sumerian ancestors and follow one of the greatest traditions in human history.

And you, dear reader, are carrying on the same tradition right now.

The rise of the machine that changed the world

In 1450 everything changed.

Revolutions in reading had occurred before, of course, driven by advancements in technology. Clay tablets were replaced by papyrus scrolls and parchment (stretched animal skins), then eventually paper became king (originally from China, as old silk and cloth were pulped and stretched). Each new material ushered in a new age of increased reading access and a vital boom in literacy.

The widespread use of paper was of course seminal to the creation of books as we now know them, but it was the machinery devised by the genius of an obscure German gem-cutter and goldsmith that truly changed the world. With the advent of the printing presses and moveable type in 1450, the Middle Ages folded and an age of discovery – founded on the growth of reading – began.

Johannes Gutenberg, from Mainz in Germany, moved the production of books from painstakingly handwritten expensive artefacts to cheap, easily replicated products. By inventing moveable type – with a collection of wooden characters (later developed to use metal) that could effectively stamp oil-based ink on paper – printing was able to copy 42 lines at once, radically speeding up the process of book production. Just as speedily, one printing press in Strasburg (where Johanne had settled) in 1450 mushroomed into 1,700 printing presses, producing 27,000 books and something like 10 million copies, a mere 30 years later. Labour-intensive handwritten books quickly became rare artefacts or died out completely.

Gutenberg himself died in 1468, in his hometown of Mainz, in relative obscurity and rumoured to have gone blind. And yet, with his groundbreaking invention, Gutenberg would ultimately make many more people in the world read and see twice as well, as Menander predicted.

The profound impact of the printing presses was swift and dramatic throughout Europe. In Germany, Martin Luther would seize upon the newly popular printed pamphlets to begin a religious revolution. William Caxton, who would bring the printing presses to England, quickly saw that English books sold better than Latin, and so these newly printed books flooding the continent would influence religion and spark the written English language into life. Religious belief and the way people lived their daily lives irrevocably changed with the invention of cheap, accessible reading.

As we know, access to books redefined education, and in turn, subsequent schooling reform transformed reading and literacy. Spurred on by Protestantism and economic expansion, alongside a wish to have more than just the clergy read the bible, schooling as we know it emerged in the sixteenth century. The children of 'commoners' – alas, again, almost exclusively boys – would see mass education begin to emerge. Grammar schools (so-called because they were characterised by a teaching of Latin grammar) were founded, funded by merchants and some enlightened members of the clergy. Now, much of the expected reading would be religious in nature, but pupils and adults would speedily seek out romances and adventure novels as an insatiable demand for reading spread across Europe and the globe.

By 1900, around 90% of English people were now functionally literate. This literacy was nourishing and perhaps more wide-ranging than many people today would expect. You can read, in Mayhew's *London Labour and the London Poor*, about thriving city libraries and intriguing stories of poor 'penny-mousetrap' makers talking of their 'hour's light reading' of Shakespeare's plays and Milton's *Paradise Lost*. A humble mousetrap maker summed it up neatly: "It gives a man a greater insight into the world and creation, and it makes his labour a pleasure and a pride to him, when he can work with his head as well as his hands."[8]

I like to imagine that the ancestors of that mousetrap maker became teachers.

In only a few hundred years then, reading and literacy became an experience for the many in England, transforming every facet of how we lived our lives at work and at play, from millionaire bankers to mousetrap makers.

Every reader of this book is the direct beneficiary of this particular story.

As a species we took around 2,000 years to move from representing objects and ideas as symbols, to devising letters and an alphabet to represent those sounds. For pupils in our classroom, we have something like 2,000 days to gain the same complex insights and knowledge to read the English language. Happily, with the advent of schools and ready access to paper books, teachers everywhere have helped pupils rise to that challenge.

Children's reading: a literature of their own

Let's begin at the beginning:

> Perhaps it is only in childhood that books have any deep influence on our lives. In later years we admire, we are entertained, we may modify some views we already hold, but we are more likely to find in books merely a confirmation of what is in our minds already.
>
> 'The Lost Childhood', by Graham Greene, p. 13[9]

It would be thousands of years before the boys of the writing houses in Sumeria, alongside the countless girls hidden from our view of history, would *eventually* be deemed fit to be taught to read and would go on to gain a literature of their own. Early in the nineteenth century, the dominant mode of reading to children was mainly for religious and moral instruction. This was finally supplanted by reading to gain any sort of knowledge and for the sheer entertainment and pleasure of it.

Many children have of course experienced the pleasure of stories since recorded history. In the ancient Greek play, *Lysistrata*, by Aristophanes, the Chorus describe "a fable they used to relate to me when I was a little boy".

Though boys and girls in ancient eras were no doubt rapt by myths, legends and tales told by family and friends, it took much longer to see such stories emerge into a literature of their own.

If you look carefully, you can see in the Greek moral fables of Aesop – as the tortoise outwitted the hare and the boy cried wolf – where in 1901 Beatrix Potter found her inspiration for her plucky rabbits. You can see in the Anglo-Saxon stories of Beowulf, how J. K. Rowling stands on the shoulders of monstrous giants. Perhaps we now take for granted the rich heritage of children's literature that can be the birthright of most of our pupils (but alas, not all).

In the centuries after printing presses emerged in England, books for children quickly developed. Usually, children were fed with dry religious primers and grammar books, but even these could have a brutal beauty for eager young readers. For example, James Janeway's *A Token for Children* (1671–1672), would offer intriguing accounts of "exemplary lives and joyful deaths of several young children". Though our own young pupils may baulk at the thought of accounts of sinful children recounting their errors and renouncing their wickedness, according to contemporary book sales, such death and doom were well received.[10]

Traditional stories told for thousands of years emerged into what we know as 'fairy tales'. The name 'fairy tale' was actually coined in seventeenth-century France ('*conte de fées*' in French) by Madame d'Aulnoy.[11] But the Disneyfied modern versions of these tall tales have darker, more graphic origins. Indeed, be careful not to read the story of Cinderella, from the Brothers Grimm, without a trigger warning about the Ugly Sister's chopping off their toes to fit into the glass slipper! In these famed fables, set 'Once Upon a Time', children would get to discover the disorientating and dangerous world of adulthood within the confines of a story.

Though many books and familiar fairy tales were written for children in the seventeenth and eighteenth centuries, the first golden age of children's reading was likely late in the nineteenth century. It was Charles Dodgson – better known by his pen name, Lewis Carroll – who would publish *Alice in Wonderland*, in 1865 (after a boat ride in Oxford, entertaining the daughters of the local Reverend Robinson Duckworth) – that would signal an end to the dominance of pious religious tales. Soon after, in 1883, Robert Louis Stevenson would publish *Treasure Island* (written to entertain his 12-year-old stepson) and it would signal the birth of adventure stories especially written for young children.

At the turn of the century, in 1901, Beatrix Potter, using the very last of her savings, wrote the first of 23 illustrated tales of Peter Rabbit. The success of these simple tales solidified the power of pictures in children's books. Though many books preceded Potter, her stories and accompanying sketches helped usher in the first century of human history that could fairly be called the 'century of reading'.

Children's books like *Peter Pan, Peter Rabbit* and *Little Women* would do more than just offer pleasure – they would come to best define our very notion of childhood. As Virginia Woolf stated, "The impressions of childhood are those that last the longest and cut the deepest."[12] These children's stories then would cut deep into our collective consciousness. While children would fly off into magical secret gardens and Neverlands, the nineteenth century would also usher in the schooling we take for granted today.

Adventure stories like *Treasure Island* would go on to be legitimised and newly studied by countless classes of boys and girls in school. As technology made books ever cheaper to produce, libraries boomed and books of every genre – fiction and non-fiction – would become an integral part of many of our children's lives (though, sadly, as we know, not all pupils gain a shelf of their own).

As we live and read now – surrounded by books and texts of all kinds: paper, digital, audio and more – with a near-endless wealth of information available through our fingertips, we could be forgiven for taking this success for granted.

We are arguably amid another golden age of children's literature, with J. K. Rowling's ubiquitous wizards (part Arthurian legend and part *Cinderella*, mixed with *Tom Brown's School Days*), alongside authors like Phillip Pullman, Katherine Rundell, Malorie Blackman and Michael Morpurgo, producing blockbuster books that morph into plays, films and minor industries. Thousands of artful picture books are now published each year for young children.

These brilliant books are also slowly beginning to reflect the realities of class and race[13] – though there is still work to do in holding a mirror to the lives of many of our pupils. If we attend to reading in school and build upon this great tradition of children's literature, such stories can act as a mirror for pupils to learn about themselves, while opening a window on the world for them too.

And yet, regardless of the wealth of literature for young people, despite the millions of available books, universal education and wide reading, we are left to question: Will our culture of children's reading as we know it be irrevocably changed by the rising tide of YouTube channels and ubiquitous technology?

The death of reading or a brave new world?

We live in an era when the act of reading is changing as rapidly as any time in its short 5,000-year-old history. In effect, we have travelled from our pupils scratching away on clay tablets to our pupils scrolling away on their electronic tablets.

In every epoch of reading new innovations change not just reading, but our very society. With the advent of mobile technology and the Internet, we are quickly chasing the story of reading through dizzyingly fast turns. A natural response to such drastic changes in how we live our lives is one of fear. It is a noble tradition – as we know – the great philosopher Socrates greatly feared how books would be a detriment to the power of both memory and speech.

Are our current worries about the act of reading being replaced by a diluted diet of speedy scrolling warranted? Should we resurrect the sceptical fears of Socrates?

Professor Maryanne Woolf, respected author and professor of education, has written sensitively about her fears of an irreversibly damaging change in our reading habits: "What concerns me as a scientist is whether expert readers like us, after multiple hours (and years) of daily screen reading, are subtly changing the allocation of attention to key processes when reading longer, more complex texts."[14] Though we are still in the midst of such seismic changes, we know that there is evidence for the limitations of technology. For a long time, we have known that television simply doesn't help us think hard, so when toddlers are developing their language, watching talk on television doesn't bring the same benefits as reading a book.[15] There is also some evidence that there is less interaction with shared reading when it is on an e-book compared to paper books.[16]

So, should we hold on to our hardbacks and put down our technological devices? We probably need to do a bit of both.

The most recent available evidence would indicate that reading from paper would offer more substantive learning than its digital counterparts, but this is more pressing under timed conditions and reading non-fiction texts.[17] Perhaps then our pupils better associate paper with learning, whereas tablets prompt a playfulness in their mind? It could be that scrolling, switching and multitasking on our devices, inhibits our attention, to echo Woolf's concerns?

Such emerging evidence poses some really useful questions for teachers:

- Are our pupils sustaining their attention when they read? How do we know?
- How effortful is our pupils' reading on technological devices? Are they skimming and skipping – and actually only reading at a surface level?
- How do we ensure our pupils are active, strategic readers, regardless of the mode of what they read?

Should we chuck out the laptops? Probably not. We cannot turn back the clock – so better training pupils in how to read in a digital space is our best bet. As teachers, we do need to consider where and when we ask pupils to screen read, or to pick up a paper book instead.

We should be wary of scaremongering about the effect of new technology, lest we repeat the mistakes of such careful commentary in centuries past. Concerned parents and teachers may be worried by the corrosive impact of *Call of Duty* or *Assassin's Creed*, but then they may be surprised to know that the latter has Umberto Eco – world renowned author – as a plot consultant.

The cultural currency of reading itself took a long time to accrue. Once upon a time, novels were frowned upon as frivolous in comparison to poetry. Fast forward a couple of hundred years: children's literature was scorned, with greats like Enid Blyton criticised for dumbing down writing, with her vocabulary attacked for its simplicity and for damaging our sensitive youngsters.

Sound familiar?

As teachers and guardians, we should be watchful about reading. The sobering reality is that it is only in the last couple of hundred years that the majority of people in the West could read and write. As such, reading *is* fragile. When I watch my own two children at home revelling in their electronic devices, I recognise the power and promise of new technology, while also recognising the vital power of deep, 'traditional' reading that proves the master skill of school.

A handy note of caution about the seeming threat to reading by our obsession with technology is posed by Edward Jenner: "It would be a shame if brilliant technology were to end up threatening the kind of intellect that produced it."[18]

Ultimately, if the story of reading has taught us anything, it is that turning points like 1450 didn't damage reading as was feared. In fact, quite the opposite. They simply consolidated it as the greatest and most important of human inventions. As our pupils journey across the near-infinite reaches of the Internet, and more, it will be the act of reading – careful, strategic and increasingly expert – that will help navigate new, exciting advancements in learning.

Put simply: reading matters more than ever.

It is reassuring that today we'll learn similarly to our Sumerian ancestors over 5,000 years ago, but that we have also learnt still further how to refine, and quietly transform, how we read and learn best to be prepared for any imminent change in our future.

A history of reading

When you envision the Sumerian classroom of the past and then think of your pupils reading and listening in the present, you can see a rich tradition, along with new challenges and opportunities (see Figure 2.4). Knowing about the history and science of reading will matter if we are to build upon that great tradition and to seize each and every new opportunity in the classroom and beyond.

IN SHORT …

- Humans have been reading for only around 5,000 years … a sliver of our evolutionary history.
- The first known reading in a school-like context was the teaching of cuneiform on clay tablets in ancient Mesopotamia (modern-day Iraq). Some of the approaches to teaching reading would prove strikingly familiar to modern day teachers.
- Texts to be read in ancient times would have proved significantly different to our contemporary notion of books. This included *scriptura continua*, with an absence of word spacing or recognisable punctuation. The formalisation of spelling and punctuation is only a few hundred years old.
- The evolution of machines has always been inextricably linked to changes and developments in reading, from the invention of paper, to the Gutenberg printing presses in the 1450s, and finally to personal computers in our modern age.
- Literature written for children has only been established in the last couple of hundred years, but it has already transformed our conceptions of childhood and of the teaching of reading.

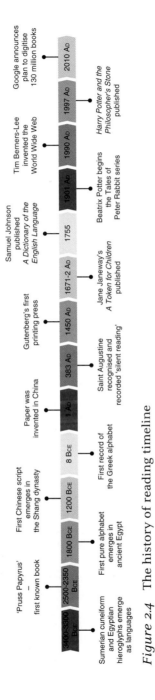

Figure 2.4 The history of reading timeline

Notes

1 Saenger, P. (1997). *Space between words: The origins of silent reading.* Stanford, CA: Stanford University Press.

2 Manguel, A. (1997). *A history of reading.* London: Flamingo, p. 43.

3 Saenger, P. (1997). *Space between words: The origins of silent reading.* Stanford, CA: Stanford University Press.

4 Manguel, A. (1997). *A history of reading.* London: Flamingo, p. 48.

5 Ibid., p. 119.

6 Shanahan, T. (2017). *What is close reading?* Retrieved from https://shanahanonliteracy.com/blog/what-is-close-reading.

7 Manguel, A. (1997). *A history of reading.* London: Flamingo.

8 Mayhew, H. (2018). *London labour and the London poor* (Vol. 3 of 4). A Project Gutenberg e-book. Retrieved from www.gutenberg.org/files/57060/57060-h/57060-h.htm#Page_43.

9 Greene, G. (1999). The lost childhood. In G. Greene, *Collected essays.* London: Vintage, p. 13.

10 Grenby, M. O. (2014). The origins of children's literature. Retrieved from www.bl.uk/romantics-and-victorians/articles/the-origins-of-childrens-literature?_ga=2.199556525.2090890301.1549926532-624299337.1549926532.

11 Oxford Reference (2017). *The tale of Madame d'Aulnoy.* Retrieved from https://blog.oup.com/2017/06/fairy-tale-of-madame-daulnoy.

12 Woolf, V. (2015). *The moment and other essays.* A Project Gutenberg e-book. Retrieved from www.gutenberg.net.au/ebooks15/1500221h.html.

13 Centre for Literacy in Primary Education (2019). *Reflecting realities: A survey of ethnic representation within UK children's literature 2018.* Retrieved from: https://clpe.org.uk/publications-and-bookpacks/reflecting-realities/reflecting-realities-survey-ethnic-representation.

14 Woolf, M. (2009). *Reader come home: The reading brain in a digital world.* New York: Harper Collins, p. 39.

15 Alloway, T. P., Williams, S., Jones, B., & Cochrane, F. (2014). Exploring the impact of television watching on vocabulary skills in toddlers. *Early Childhood Education Journal, 42*(5), 343–349.

16 Munzer, T. G., Miller, A. L., Weeks, H. M., Kaciroti, N., & Radesky, J. (2019). Differences in parent–toddler interactions with electronic versus print books. *Pediatrics, 143*(4), e20182012. doi:10.1542/peds.2018-2012.
17 Delgado, P., Vargas, C., Ackerman, R., & Salmerón, L. (2018). Don't throw away your printed books: A meta-analysis on the effects of reading media on reading comprehension. *Educational Research Review, 25*, 23–38.
18 Tenner, E. (2006). Searching for dummies. *New York Times.* Retrieved from www.nytimes.com/2006/03/26/opinion/searching-for-dummies.html.

3 A scientific eye on reading

The act of reading is such an integral part of the fabric of our lives – indeed, part of ourselves – that we can take it for granted. Given its personal nature, too much scientific analysis of the act of reading itself can feel like an attempt to unweave the rainbow. Crucially then, we should show every teacher how such attention on the science of reading can shine an invaluable light on how our pupils learn.

Take one of the most famous openings in English literature and give it a read:

> It was a bright cold day in April, and the clocks were striking thirteen. Winston Smith, his chin nuzzled into his breast in an effort to escape the vile wind, slipped quickly through the glass doors of Victory Mansions.
>
> *1984*, by George Orwell, p. 1[1]

As your eye movement scanned the first sentence, each word received a mere 250 milliseconds of fame.[2] You then seemingly read each word of both sentences fluently and in a regular rhythm, moving quickly like the character of Winston.

For an experienced reader, we near-effortlessly match letters to sounds. We then draw upon a wealth of connected knowledge of words, phrases, syntax (the order and structure of the sentences) and countless linguistic patterns – sounding out while making sense of things. When individual words violate our sensitivity to our fluent pattern-making processes – like a clock striking "thirteen" – we monitor our thinking and reading, speedily repairing and revisiting what we know from our vast store of background knowledge.

We can decode all of the words and make sense of them in order, before cohering the author's clever and odd use of "thirteen" and it signalling the novel taking place in an unfamiliar world – triggering its relation to the wider genre of dystopian fiction.

The science of reading then can help us chart the intricate path from reading simple words like 'cold' and 'day' to comprehending infinitely complex stories that describe imagined worlds, and much more. Whether familiar to you or not, reading this novel opening sees you enact a process of dazzling complexity. Indeed, 'real' reading is so complex and multifaceted, that it is hard to study, so we deconstruct it into its component parts, such as decoding – synthesising the component sounds of words – word recognition, fluency and reading comprehension, etc.

Our brain has acquired the ability to read by drawing upon our spoken language – our grasp of sound and speech – but translating those speech sounds to their corresponding written code is when everything gets tricky. As renowned cognitive psychologist Stephen Pinker stated, "Children are wired for sound, but print is an optional accessory that must be painstakingly bolted on."[3] We therefore need to be explicit and skilful about how we teach that code-breaking act in school, until it appears more *natural*.

Given the English language has borrowed and stolen words from around 350 languages[4] from all around the globe, for thousands of years, it has developed a complex code. Given the English language has three times as many words than there are in the German language and six times as many as in French[5] – oh, and most of those words are polysemous[6] (individual words that have multiple potential meanings) and have different spelling patterns – code-breaking proves a difficult challenge. There is simply so much language we need to store in our brain to access reading that it proves a life-long pursuit.

Is it any wonder reading skill in English takes twice as long to develop compared to 'simpler' languages?[7]

So why do so many adults perceive reading to be natural and relatively easy? Well, we could describe this as the 'expert car-driver effect'. Even soon after qualifying as a roadworthy driver, we quickly automate the painful novice steps of changing gears, checking our mirrors, reading the road and much more. The driving process merges into a cohesive, apparently fluent skill, just like reading can feel to almost all literate adults.

When it comes to learning to read, it just isn't as natural or easy as learning to speak (though that proves difficult for some too), so simply reading great books to our children – valuable though it no doubt proves – invariably won't prove enough. In a related research study of reading with preschoolers, the children spent 20 times longer looking at the pictures in the storybook that was being read than they did looking at the words[8] (quite rightly, I may add). They just didn't *naturally* read the words.

In other evidence, many young children assume that their parents are actually using the pictures to read to them rather than the inky squiggles.[9] Staring at the shapes of letters is something that children begin to properly appreciate after lots and lots of reading practice and teaching that makes this appear to happen intuitively.

Without doubt, the reading environment in the home, alongside an exposure to rich talk (that is to say, lots of turn taking and engagement in extended talk), before children ever get to school, holds significant value[10] and offers the critical foundations for school and reading success. Crucially, however, for the majority of children, they'll still require lots of strategic instruction to learn to read and to go on to 'read to learn'. It will likely prove more than we assume, for longer than we expect.

To return to the driving analogy, we know, often via frightening realisations, that not every qualified driver on our roads is very good at driving! Many of our novice pupils struggle along the road of reading too.

Some parents and teachers rightly cite their own experience of learning to read quite *naturally* and without much formal instruction at all. Such anecdotes are often used to challenge the formal instruction of phonics or reading comprehension strategies early on at school. Now, investigations into what are termed 'precocious readers'[11] have shown that some children are untypical in their development. These children, likely through exposure to ample reading at home, and lots of rich exposure to talk and language, very speedily grasp phonic patterns and read with a fluency that belies their years.

Structured phonics instruction, or deliberate attention-to-reading strategies, would appear to be not wholly necessary then for these precocious readers. These children are in part self-taught already and so the repetition of 'basic' reading strategies could be deemed dull. Parents can then understandably get frustrated when this is the case. And yet, we are talking about a small minority of readers. For most children, explicit, structured and sustained reading instruction – early and for an extended period that spans primary *and* secondary school – is essential for success. Let's gift our pupils with this key to crack the reading code.

If teachers are supported to develop their knowledge of reading – a troublesome gap if it is absent – then we can deftly navigate the reading needs of *every* pupil in our classrooms.

Why all the fuss about phonics?

Let's begin at the beginning. Very young children are wired for sound. Before children ever get to school, they are indirectly honing their preparedness to be readers. The capacity to read words on the page sits upon the experience of every shared story,[12] meaningful conversations[13] and fun singalongs.

As reading researcher Maryanne Woolf emphasises, the system of sounds that makes up the words we read (the branch of language study known as *phonology*) is fundamental for reading success:

> Extensive research on the development of this phonological aspect of language indicates that systematic play with rhymes, first sounds, and last sounds in wordplay, jokes and songs significantly contributes to a child's readiness to learn to read. Teaching a child to enjoy poetry and music is serious child's play.
>
> *Proust and the Squid,* by Maryanne Woolf, p. 100[14]

As small children begin to read the world around them – before they can read words on the page – they can make sense of visual cues, such as 'reading' common signs. And so, a child could recognise and remember a roadside 'Stop' sign, but it is the visual memory of the colours and symbols that allows the child to 'read' (termed the pre-alphabetic stage[15]) and not their ability to decode letters into sounds. It is the next vital stage – the recognition that letters can translate into sounds – which is vital for 'real' reading.

Young pupils have to learn to grapple with the alphabetic code: deciphering letter patterns and converting them into sounds. This process is underpinned by our pupils' 'phonological awareness'. That is to say, their ability to recognise individual sounds – compare them, isolate them and more. Effectively, there are 44 phonemes in the English language that map on to our English alphabet, as shown in the Appendix.

Children with good phonological awareness can answer simple, but fundamental, questions about the sounds in the words they read. A pupil isolating a phoneme would be able to answer the question: what sound does the word 'from' begin with? A pupil being able to match phonemes would be able to answer the question: Which word begins with the same sound as 'bed'? 'Cart, shard or beach'? Rhyming patterns are easily discerned. These are apparently simple steps in early language acquisition, but they prove critical and not every child acquires them quickly and confidently.

The common practice of teaching phonics in English schools is founded upon a broad scientific consensus that helping our pupils crack the alphabetic code requires systematic teaching.[16] A handy summary is that the teaching of structured phonics is "helpful for all children, harmful for none, and crucial for some".[17]

Put simply, phonics is the method of instruction that explicitly teaches pupils to map sounds (phonemes) on to their corresponding letters (graphemes). For example, the word 'shop' has four letters but only three phonemes: 'sh' – 'o' – 'p'. 'Sh' is labelled in the phonetic alphabet as /ʃ/. The 44 phonemes in the phonetic alphabet should be taught systematically, so that pupils can move to decoding automatically.

In England, the government-favoured method is 'synthetic phonics'. This is a method characterised by separating letter sounds, before blending them together: b – a – t – creating bat. The other main approach is 'analytic phonics', which begins with studying the word and then identifying the composite phonemes. The process sees whole words analysed, so a pupil may identify the word 'hid', with the 'id' sound isolated, then other words created such as 'bid' and 'did'.

So, what is all the fuss about?

For well over 100 years, arguments about the value of phonics has raged. Indeed, in the United States, back in 1843, the very emphasis on words broken down into their composite parts was described as "skeleton-shaped, bloodless, ghostly apparitions".[18] It was argued this would no doubt quash pupils' motivation and interest in reading.

Over time, duelling sides emerged and a century has passed with the fighting still ongoing. The 'phonics' camp became widely opposed by the proponents of 'whole language'. Those who backed 'whole language' deemed phonics reductive and instead prioritised a focus on whole words and real reading experiences. These, it is believed, will promote the necessary motivation lacked by pursuing the "ghostly" phonics method.

Despite there being a scientific consensus that structured phonics is the most efficient method of instruction (with synthetic phonics being recommended by some researchers as easier to start with young pupils[19]), it is obvious that contentious debates have trumped the reading science. These debates have proven so vehement that they have been termed the 'reading wars'.[20]

Perhaps an illustrative example about why these 'reading wars' still rage, even though the reading scientists would predominantly favour the phonics method first, is the aforementioned 'phonics check' in England. This national assessment, conducted in year 1, involves 40 words for children to decode – 20 real words and 20 non-words (or 'alien words'). Real words like 'chop' and 'sing' are tested alongside words like 'skap' and 'blorn'.[21] Many parents of competent young readers understandably can't grasp why their child would read and slip up on a word like 'blorn', when they are reading relatively well at home. To a parent, it is understandably rather jarring.

The example of the 'phonics check' reveals parents with lived experiences that clash with the more technical science of reading. The focus of the assessment is intent on isolating and diagnosing pupils' ability to decode. 'Alien words' (or 'monster words') then remove the pupil's ability to guess words based on their familiarity, which is related to their frequently appearing in school texts, etc. So then, such alien words make for a more accurate assessment of the pupil's decoding skill. Is this rationale communicated well to parents?

As the 'phonics check' proves high stakes for schools, in a long-established culture of high accountability, preparation can overreach and pupils can end up wrongly being taught alien words, while the pass mark becomes a de facto target for many schools. The 'phonics check' could arguably leave little space for vocabulary checks, or important attention on reading comprehension. Many a teacher would argue that national testing then can poison attitudes towards issues related to the science of reading.

We know that phonics alone would prove insufficient in our aim to develop pupils as flourishing readers. In reality, it will only comprise around 20 to 30 minutes of a child's school day in early primary school. What else happens inside and outside of the classroom in these school years will also prove important.

We know that regularly reading with adults – and other rich language experiences – are crucial factors in securing successful readers[22] (where phonics is unlikely to feature prominently). And yet, this is another singular support factor that will not prove enough in isolation. Rhyming, reciting poetry, singing and talking will all contribute to supporting reading, but these will not prove enough in isolation either.

Complex challenges require complex solutions.

Given reading is such a complex, multifaceted skill, it is no surprise that it will require significant support, with multiple aids, for most pupils. A structured approach to phonics just happens to be a highly efficient method to jump-start an important facet of reading development early and quickly. While it is successful in helping our pupils crack the academic code, no reading scientist would consider phonics teaching without a concurrent teaching focus on reading fluency, motivation, comprehension and more.

As most parents, and many teachers, are typically untrained in the science of early reading, resistance can build against related practices like structured phonics. We can put it in simple terms though, for every teacher and parent: phonological awareness and phonic knowledge is foundational. If a child cannot decode the word 'photosynthesis', there is a clear issue with accessing the school curriculum. Decoding, or more simply 'word-reading', skill is a prerequisite step for every pupil's reading success.

Reading fast or reading fluently?

The 'science of reading' can often be ignored because it is simply too complex and commonly held simple myths about reading go on to trump the contested science. Our personal experiences of reading can prove more significant to us than the tricky, and sometimes obscure, science too. It is only by challenging established truths and questioning our personal assumptions that we'll go on to learn what every teacher needs to know about the complex, vital act of reading.

One of the biggest reading myths we can bust is the notion that we can 'speed-read'. Thousands of adverts attest to this commonplace myth. Like most myths, there are grains of truth from which salesmen have built flimsy sandcastles in the air.

Try answering the following question:

How many animals did Moses bring on to the Ark?

So, did you guess the answer? Take a look at the end of the chapter to find out.* This is a simple example of how the very notion of speed-reading is problematic and doesn't offer our pupils, or earnest adults, much to go on regarding getting better at the complicated act of learning.

The huge promise of speed-reading ultimately proves illusory. The typical reading rate is about 240 words per minute.[23] If you wanted to, you could skim through a couple of thousand words in that time – rapidly flicking through pages. You may manage to decode some of the words, but you wouldn't likely be fully comprehending what you have read, unless it is a really easy text, and then this probably wouldn't appear in the classroom.

When you are reading significantly quicker than 240 words per minute you aren't *really* reading. You would instead be *skimming* (reading quickly to secure a general idea of what is being read) or *scanning* (reading to find some specific information). These are eminently useful reading strategies. They can help you locate some important information, but it wouldn't likely secure deep comprehension of whole texts. The real goal of reading is comprehension, and to gain such an understanding of what we have read requires slower, effortful attention.

What can the speediest of real readers realistically achieve? The fastest recorded adult readers with comprehension can reach around 600 words a minute.[24] However, like the aforementioned 'precocious readers', it doesn't offer teachers much useful guidance for the teaching of reading. For almost all classroom reading tasks, speed-reading will prove plain unhelpful. We are better off with concentrating on the relatively slow, deliberate process of reading for meaning. Then we need to understand the subtle difference between reading speedily and reading with fluency.

One reason for the common myth of speed-reading is that we can mistake the relative speed of an adult reader, or an older pupil, for what we would more precisely term 'reading fluency'. Fluent readers no longer need to slow … ly … de … code in … div … id … u … al sounds in words because they recognise words automatically. As they free up mental bandwidth by making such word reading automatic, they have more space to consider the meaning of the language and go on to put the appropriate expression in their voice, etc. Their reading begins to sound 'natural', akin to how they may speak, with their pacing sounding like typical talk.

Instead of reading really quickly – as promoted by speed-reading salesmen – we should promote fluent reading in the classroom.[25]

Reading fluency will sound distinctive when we listen to our pupils read aloud. Their reading will have elements of expressiveness, their volume and phrasing will skilfully match what is being read and they will read with a smoothness and an appropriate pace.[26] Reading as fast as a machine gun is seldom appropriate. A further challenge is that some pupils can read with better expression than their peers, but it doesn't guarantee they are comprehending what they read (more on that in the next chapter).

See the four aspects of reading fluency, which are adapted from Professor Timothy Rasinski's 'multidimensional fluency scale':[27]

1. **Expression and volume**: the varying of expression and volume to match the interpretation of the passage being read.
2. **Phrasing**: the reading of words and clauses with appropriate pauses, with an awareness of reading mostly in clauses and sentences over individual words.
3. **Smoothness**: any breaks or difficulty in reading are resolved with self-correction.
4. **Pace**: an even, conversational reading rhythm.

See the Appendix at the end of the book for a full 'multidimensional fluency scale rubric' that has been adapted for teachers to use as a diagnostic tool.

Teachers of younger children are invariably experienced at teaching pupils to become more fluent readers. Strategies such as providing regular reading practice is obvious, alongside rereading a range of texts, promoting paired reading and choral reading (see Chapter 7 for more). Selecting short reading passages for practice is most common, building up pupils' reading stamina, while offering repeated practice where they can focus on each aspect of fluent reading. The teacher role in providing scaffolding for this process is key.

We know that for a child to read a text independently, they need to read with around 95% word-reading accuracy.[28] If the text is too difficult, then they will have to concentrate too much on recognising the words, etc. and so it no longer offers useful practice for developing fluency. Picking 'Goldilocks texts' – *not too hard, not too easy, but just right* – proves essential for classroom reading and for supporting reading at home, from reception to the furthest reaches of secondary school.

Just how many words a minute determines reading fluency for our pupils is a tricky question. The Department for Education deems the 'expected standard' for reading fluency in terms of 'words per minute' as 90 words for 7-year-olds.[29] Estimates from the United States describe a norm of around 200 words a minute being read on average by the highest 10% of 11-year-olds.[30] Such numbers are rough approximations that could be useful indicators, as long as they are used intelligently.

Teachers should be aware of other important factors at play: the difficulty of a text would impact on the number of words read in a minute, alongside the purpose of the reading matter. And so, if pupils are aiming to read for a quick gist, they'll read more in that short minute than if they were reading (and likely rereading) a complex mathematics problem.

Almost every teacher, not wholly confident in the science of reading, can recognise a reader who lacks fluency. Simply sitting down with a pupil for a couple of minutes can offer enough to begin to judge fluency issues, judging their pace, phrasing and volume, alongside their words per minute. Though fluency doesn't guarantee full comprehension of what is read, it really does matter, so we need to know more about it.

With a greater understanding of the science of reading, we needn't be seduced by the myth of speed and we should instead prioritise the development of reading with fluency for pupils across the phases, from 5 to 15 years of age.

All eyes on reading

The more we learn about the science of reading the more illusions we shatter and the better it informs how we should teach our pupils at every phase. Each insight offers us a tangible nudge that can help us better diagnose when a pupil is not reading successfully, as much as steer us towards prompts about what influences we can, and cannot, exert upon our pupils' reading.

Let's return to the previous section of the book that you have just read. It poses a significant burden on your combined reading skill. Do you feel confident you have synthesised and comprehended its meaning? How about we reflect upon the words that you *really* read and those that you didn't? Could you describe 'reading fluency' to a friend with confidence? Did you think you read every word with equal attention?

Evidence on the eye movements we undertake as we read reach back well over a century. In 1908, Edmund Huey developed a device that could track eye movement during reading. Another reading myth was challenged: we don't read anywhere near as smoothly as we think.

The smoothness and fluency of a mature reader simply belie the truth hidden in our eyes. Instead, as we read, we make quick, jumpy movements – called 'saccades' (which last around 20–40 milliseconds) – mixed with micro pauses on individual words and letters – named 'fixations' (which last around 200–250 milliseconds). To use another driving analogy, in describing eye movements, we read like a new driver trying to drive a car for the first time, but repeatedly stuttering and halting. We just do all of this in a matter of milliseconds.

The average saccade is around seven to eight letters and, rather oddly, our vision is actually suppressed during this time. And so, our reading looks rather different slowed down to accurately represent how we really read:

The way our (eyes move) as we (read books) proves (surprising) to many and requires (evidence.)

Now, for young, novice readers – or older readers who struggle – their reading proves slow and they average more fixations than good readers, as they painstakingly piece together letters into sounds and attempt to recognise whole words, phrases and sentences.[31] The more complex the sentence structure for our young readers, the more the fixations.[32] Their saccades also jump back more often to words they struggled with – labelled 'regressions'. The weaker the reader, the greater the number of regressions.

The science of eye movements during reading helps to describe, at a micro level, the barriers to fluency described in the previous section. If you sit next to a pupil who struggles with reading, this jumpy, dysfluent process becomes more obvious. You can hear it in their slow, staccato rhythm. With very specialist equipment, you can also see it in their eye movements.

We know that eye movements aren't considered the cause of reading difficulties – but instead they indicate when a pupil has barriers to reading. On average, eye fixations greatly improve at around 8 to 10 years of age, reaching adult levels at around 11 years of age.[33] As pupils read more, fixation duration decreases, saccade length increases and there are fewer regressions. However, skilled adult readers still spend longer reading low frequency, tricky words, while making more regressions with complex sentence structures.[34]

The eye-movement process gets smoother when what is termed the 'self-teaching mechanism' kicks in. This describes how pupils use their word-reading skills to sound out and process new words with increasing independence. With well-targeted practice, reading speed and reading skill rapidly increase because word recognition happens near instantly. Good readers tend to then skip some function words and fixate upon nouns and verbs in sentences without it impairing their comprehension greatly. We become *speedy*, skilled readers, without the gross exaggerations promised by 'speed-reading'.

The more you read then the better you recognise words and our eye movements become seemingly smoother and more fluent (though nothing like speed-reading). Letter combinations and patterns become more visible. It is why long words like 'recontestable' can be rapidly processed even if we don't grasp the meaning instantly as we read, but 'izbqatstcoenr' stops us in our tracks and proves more effortful. Reading becomes a process of rapid pattern recognition that is greatly aided by practice. In short, we 'chunk' letters together, then words, before chunking words into common phrases and so on.

Try reading the following sentences from the history curriculum:

> The Industrial Revolution was a seminal moment in the history of the United Kingdom. This period, spanning the eighteenth and nineteenth century, marked a shift from an agrarian, rural society to an industrial and urban society.

Now, consider more carefully how you read this short passage that would be pretty indicative of GCSE informational texts. Once our pupils can decode individual words, becoming a fluent reader then shifts to reading phrases with smoothness and an appropriate emphasis. Revisit the passage and consider what the phrases you identified to read 'naturally' together are. Were the phrases you identified similar to this?

> The **Industrial Revolution** was a **seminal moment** in the **history of the United Kingdom**. This period, spanning the **eighteenth and nineteenth century**,

marked a shift from an **agrarian, rural society** to an **industrial and urban society**.

These natural *chunks* of language typically attend the important nouns and verbs in the sentence. Lots of nouns come in recognisable pairs or phrases (labelled a 'compound noun') such as 'Industrial Revolution' and 'United Kingdom'. You can see this in many school subjects, so in art a pupil would be expected to understand and use 'abstract expressionism', or 'transition metals' and 'ionic bonds' in science. Not only that, many of the sayings and idioms we use also offer us recognisable phrases e.g. 'peace and quiet' (named idiomatic pairs). With reading practice, these become more readily recognised. Reading quickly becomes a smoother sounding, fluent process for most of our pupils.

Teachers keeping a close eye on reading

So, what can teachers do?

Are there eye exercises for struggling readers? Well, no. There is no quick-fix eye-movement exercise we can practise to make our pupils more fluent readers. The only available answer for teachers here is nurturing reading experience, with appropriate guidance and lots of it, while recognising when typical reading isn't occurring when it should normally develop. We can make visible the important chunks of every text we read with pupils. We can nurture more fluent reading by encouraging pupils to cluster words into phrases and to convey that in their expression when reading aloud. Of course, pupils will need practice in reading aloud.

Teachers need to nurture the motivation of pupils as they grapple with the frustrations of their slow, effortful reading. By selecting rich texts in the classroom to read to pupils, we can introduce new, challenging vocabulary and language, while modelling the strategies a more mature reader undertakes with seeming effortlessness. Vitally, we need to nurture the delicate process of 'self-teaching' by encouraging new, harder reading of 'Goldilocks books': those texts that aren't too hard, so as to quash motivation, but not too easy, so as to not introduce more complex language. As you would expect, if we are explicitly teaching a text, we can raise the difficulty bar of a chosen text considerably higher with skilful instruction.

For my own son, Noah, when he was 7 years of age, it was nurturing his obsession with the *Beast Quest* series that gave him the motivation, and practice, to rapidly increase his reading fluency and skill. This (near-endless) fantasy series was a boon in so many ways. The narrative structure was consistent with every book – with familiar heroes and villains, alongside sentences and phrases being regularly recycled ("while there is blood in my veins!" was read/shouted with great energy by us both). Though the structure was reassuringly familiar, the relatively sophisticated vocabulary and sentence structures offered an ideal 'Goldilocks degree of challenge' for my own little emerging reader. At once, Noah vanquished his monsters and began to master the vital skill of independent reading.

For my 10-year-old daughter, Freya, it is a judicious mix of reading *Harry Potter* and also non-fiction series, such as the Usborne *100 Things to Know About ...* series, along with the *Rebel Girls* books, that maintains her motivation in the face of manifold reading challenges. In these informational texts, there is a diversity of specialist vocabulary and varied text structures (diagrams and graphics) that offer the requisite 'Goldilocks degree of challenge' for her reading development.

Many secondary school teachers will be familiar with teens who struggle with reading as much as emerging 7-year-old readers. Of course, for a teenager who struggles to read, they can be hardened by successive failures. Each daily loss in the classroom can leave any notion of reading for pleasure in tatters. A vicious cycle ensues: reading is deemed frustrating and boring – reading practice is avoided – and so the frustration and failure continue. Given the greatest challenge of secondary school is academic reading, it is no wonder that those pupils who cannot read are those most likely to be destined for academic failure.

We should ask simple, but vital questions: What are the 'Goldilocks books' for year 2, year 5 and year 9? How will we mediate their complexity, while keeping an eye on the detail of our pupils' reading development?

Whether we are teachers looking to hone our practice, or parents looking to nurture the skill and will to read, we need to understand the foundations of reading, along with the barriers and necessary supports.

IN SHORT …

- The act of reading is dizzyingly complex, but as it is processed in a matter of milliseconds, we can take it for granted as a simple act.
- The science of reading has been beset by over a century of debate and arguments that are termed the 'reading wars'. Much of the debate attends the role of phonics as a method of early reading. Though some 'precocious children' may not require phonics instruction, it is likely to prove "helpful for all children, harmful for none, and crucial for some".[35]

- Reading fluency is foundational for successful reading, but it is more than simply reading fast (indeed, 'speed-reading' is a myth). Our eye movements develop as we learn to read, and our reading fluency develops concurrently. Some pupils may require explicit instruction to support them to read fluently.

- Teachers need to attend to foundational processes like word reading and reading fluency, while maintaining our pupils' motivations to read. Apt reading selections for our pupils can nurture reading practice, developing fluency, which further enhances reading motivation.

- How many animals did Moses bring on to the ark? Well, none! It was Noah who was the famed ark owner. This small error – aptly named the 'Moses illusion' – reveals how we are bedevilled by mental shortcuts, and that if we speed-read, we compromise on comprehension. We are not in fact reading; we are merely skimming the text.

Notes

1 Orwell, G. (1949). *1984*. London: Penguin.
2 Woolf, M. (2008). *Proust and the squid: The story and science of the reading brain.* Cambridge, UK: Icon Books.
3 Pinker, S., & McGuiness, D. (1998). *Why children can't read and what we can do about it.* London: Penguin, p. ix.
4 Dictionary.com (2018). Which words did English take from other languages? Retrieved from www.dictionary.com/e/borrowed-words.
5 Bromley, K. (2007). Nine things every teacher should know about words and vocabulary instruction. *Journal of Adolescent & Adult Literacy, 50*(7), 528–537.

6 Tennant, W. (2014). *Understanding reading comprehension: Processes and practices.* London: Sage.

7 Linguists describe languages as having either a shallow orthography (sounds and letters match consistently, e.g. Spanish and Finnish) or a deep orthography (sounds and letters are not consistently matched, e.g. English). Languages like English, which have a deep orthography, are harder to learn to read.

8 Ann Evans, M., & Saint-Aubin, J. (2005). What children are looking at during shared storybook reading: Evidence from eye-movement monitoring. *Psychological Science, 16*(11), 913–920. https://doi.org/10.1111/j.1467-9280.2005.01636.x.

9 Ferreiro, E., & Teberosky, A. (1982). *Literacy before schooling.* Portsmouth, NH: Heinemann Educational Books.

10 Hamilton, L. G., Hayiou-Thomas, M. E., Hulme, C., & Snowling, M. J. (2016). The home literacy environment as a predictor of the early literacy development of children at family risk of dyslexia. *Scientific Studies of Reading, 20*(5), 401–419. doi:10.1080/10888438.2016.1213266.

11 Olson, L. A., Evans, J. R., & Keckler, W. T. (2006). Precocious readers: Past, present, and future. *Journal for the Education of the Gifted, 30*(2), 205–235. https://doi.org/10.4219/jeg-2006-260.

12 Law, J., Charlton, J., McKean, C., Beyer, F., Fernandez-Garcia, C., Mashayekhi, A. & Rush, R. (2018). *Parent–child reading to improve language development and school readiness: A systematic review and meta-analysis (final report).* Newcastle and Edinburgh: Newcastle University and Queen Margaret University.

13 Snowling, M., Hulme, C., Bailey, A., Stothard, S., & Lindsay, G. (2011). *Better communication research programme: Language and literacy attainment of pupils during early years and through KS2: Does teacher assessment at five provide a valid measure of children's current and future educational attainments?* Department for Education Research Report, 172a. London: Department for Education.

14 Woolf, M. (2008). *Proust and the squid: The story and science of the reading brain.* Cambridge, UK: Icon Books.

15 Ehri, L. C., & McCormick, S. (1998). Phrases of word learning: Implications for instruction with delayed and

disabled readers. *Reading & Writing Quarterly, 14*(2), 135–163. doi:10.1080/1057356980140202.

16 Ibid.

17 Snow, C. E., & Juel, C. (2005). Teaching children to read: What do we know about how to do it? In M. J. Snowling & C. Hulme (Eds.), *The science of reading: A handbook* (pp. 501–520). Malden, MA: Blackwell.

18 Seidenberg, M. (2013). The science of reading and its educational implications. *Language Learning and Development, 9*(4): 331–360. doi:10.1080/15475441.2013.812017.

19 Shanahan, T. (2018). Which is best? Analytic or synthetic phonics? Retrieved from www.readingrockets.org/blogs/ shanahan-literacy/which-best-analytic-or-synthetic-phonics.

20 Castles, A., Rastle, K., & Nation, K. (2018). Ending the reading wars: Reading acquisition from novice to expert. *Psychological Science in the Public Interest, 19*(1), 5–51. https://doi.org/10.1177/1529100618772271.

21 Department for Education (2018). *2018 national curriculum assessments: Key stage 1 phonics screening check, national assessments.* Retrieved from https://assets. publishing.service.gov.uk/government/uploads/system/ uploads/attachment_data/file/715823/2018_phonics_pupils_ materials_standard.pdf.pdf.

22 Mol, S. E., Bus, A. G., de Jong, M. T., & Smeets, D. J. H. (2008). Added value of dialogic parent–child book readings: A meta-analysis. *Early Education and Development, 19*(1), 7–26. doi:10.1080/10409280701838603.

23 Brysbaert, M. (2019). How many words do we read per minute? A review and meta-analysis of reading rate. https:// doi.org/10.31234/osf.io/xynwg. PsyArXiv preprint.

24 Carver, R. (1992). Reading rate: Theory, research, and practical implications. *Journal of Reading, 36*(2), 84–95.

25 Rasinski, T. V., Rikli, A., & Johnston, S. (2009). Reading fluency: More than automaticity? More than a concern for the primary grades? *Literacy Research and Instruction, 48*(4), 350–361. doi:10.1080/19388070802468715.

26 Rasinski, T. V. (2006). Reading fluency instruction: Moving beyond accuracy, automaticity, and prosody. *The Reading Teacher, 59*, 704–706.

27 Rasinski, T. V., & Padak, N. (2005). *Three-minute reading assessments: Word recognition, fluency, and comprehension for grades 1–4.* New York, NY: Scholastic; Rasinski, T. V., & Cheesman Smith, M. (2018). *The megabook of fluency.* New York, NY: Scholastic.

28 Texas Education Agency (n.d.). Fluency: Instructional guidelines and student activities. Retrieved from www.reading rockets.org/article/fluency-instructional-guidelines-and-student-activities.

29 Department for Education (2018). *2018 key stage 1 teacher assessment exemplification: English reading – working at the expected standard.* Retrieved from https://assets. publishing.service.gov.uk/government/uploads/system/ uploads/attachment_data/file/762975/2018_key_stage_1_ teacher_assessment_exemplification_expected_standard. pdf.

30 Hasbrouck, J., & Tindal, G. (2017). *An update to compiled ORF norms (technical report no. 1702).* Eugene, OR. Behavioral Research and Teaching, University of Oregon.

31 Blythe, H., & Joseph, H. S. S. (2011). Children's eye movements during reading. In S. P. Liversedge, I. Gilchrist, & S. Everling (Eds.), *The Oxford handbook of eye movements* (pp. 643–662). Oxford: Oxford University Press.

32 Rayner, K., & Duffy, A. (1986). Lexical complexity and fixation times in reading: Effects of word frequency, verb complexity, and lexical ambiguity. *Memory and Cognition, 14,* 191–201.

33 Blythe, H., & Joseph, H. S. S. (2011). Children's eye movements during reading. In S. P. Liversedge, I. Gilchrist, & S. Everling (Eds.), *The Oxford handbook of eye movements* (pp. 643–662). Oxford: Oxford University Press.

34 Warren, T., White, S. J., & Reichie, E. D. (2005). Investigating the causes of wrap-up effects: Evidence from eye movements and E–Z reader. *Cognition, 111,* 132–137.

35 Snow, C. E., & Juel, C. (2005). Teaching children to read: What do we know about how to do it? In M. J. Snowling & C. Hulme (Eds.), *The science of reading: A handbook* (pp. 501–520). Malden, MA: Blackwell.

4 Reading comprehension

It is a unique privilege for a teacher to support their pupils in reading to explore the world, in both fiction and a range of informational texts. Whether it is reading about venturing into Tom's nineteenth-century midnight garden in year 6, or reading about earthquakes in New Zealand in an A level geography classroom, each pupil will require their very own world of words and background knowledge to help them make sense of their new adventures.

This quest for comprehension ultimately begins at birth. In the snug embrace of a parent, or caregiver, a child looks at a picture book and begins building their knowledge of communication and their understanding of print on a page. Though it may not appear so, a very young child pointing at an image in a picture book is an important precursor[1] to their later ability to grapple with graphs in a geography textbook. With too little experience of early shared reading and talk attending to understanding letters, words and stories, a damaging gap can quickly emerge with implications for teachers teaching in the classroom.

With each conversation about a book, alongside each question and conversational turn, children develop their listening comprehension and their language, which is the very platform for later reading comprehension. Without those rich language experiences early on, we can predict that gaps will emerge in later reading.

This delicate development of reading comprehension then encompasses broader experiences of talk and listening. We should therefore tend to oral language development in our classrooms. Each interaction between teacher and pupil can lift the print from the page and make it better understood. It is why reading, and talking about reading, needs to play a fundamental role in *every* school day.

To simplify – without making reading unrealistically simple – we can share examples that help us better grasp the complexity of reading comprehension.

A helpful illustrative example of how the complex act of reading is dependent upon our family context – alongside a delicate balancing act of different reading skills being developed and integrated – is the tale of the great English poet John Milton.[2] As an elderly man losing his sight, he asked his two daughters to read to him the Greek and Latin classics. Though they could decode the Greek words, they couldn't comprehend what was being read to their demanding grandfather. Conversely, Milton couldn't decode the words on the page, but he could listen and comprehend.

The famous Milton family anecdote mimics the complex, interrelated nature of the essential reading skills so crucial to all successful readers. It also reveals how dependent reading comprehension can be on talk – which reminds us how reading emerged primarily as an act to be spoken. The tale may also make us mindful of the value of family support factors in helping us become successful readers.

Where then do we see the gap between reading words and a deep, meaningful comprehension of what is being read in each of our classrooms?

As an English teacher, a vivid memory was being asked by a baffled and incredulous teen: "Why would Wordsworth bother to write an entire poem about daffodils?" I noted a significant comprehension gap (in many cases, such miscomprehension quickly leads to dimmed motivation). The self-same pupil could read Wordsworth's poem aloud with a degree of fluency, but then fail to appreciate the poet's use of analogy, allusions and references to Romantic symbols and ideas.

The act of reading, connecting and integrating what you read into your vast store of background knowledge of words, linguistic patterns and text structures, can happen in a mere moment. For a Wordsworth expert, the mere mention of a daffodil triggers a huge – and pleasurable – array of connections and insights. As such, reading comprehension can prove vast, diverse and therefore devilishly hard to pin down and assess. We can only "observe indirect symptoms"[3] of said comprehension. We can however see it more readily when it breaks down in the classroom. I can testify to my teaching of 'Daffodils', and many other poems, drawing confused blank faces despite my very best teaching attempts.

How can we then navigate a classroom when our pupils' prior knowledge proves lacking? How much do pupils need to know to access a challenging text – aged 6 or 16? And what tools do they need to grapple with a text when they simply don't bring enough background knowledge to reading it?

The wonder of windmills

A powerful example that brought the comprehension gap most vividly home to me was undertaking a reading homework with my son. When he was aged 6, Noah was given a reading comprehension homework task. The book, *Katje the Windmill Cat*, written by Gretchen Woefle, set 500 years ago, posed significant problems for my own young reader, who was still grappling with word reading and reading with some degree of fluency.

Take a look at part of the opening paragraph he read:

> Katje had an easy life. She lived with Nico the miller in a Dutch village by the sea. While Nico ground grain in his windmill, Katje chased mice. Up and down the ladders she prowled, searching behind sacks of grain and along beams dusty with flour.
>
> *Katje the Windmill Cat*, by Gretchen Woefle, p. 3[4]

Now, consider what words and background knowledge from this text would challenge a typical 6-year-old reader. Just considering vocabulary as one important facet of reading comprehension, how many words do you think inhibited Noah's comprehension?

It was quite clear that words and phrases like "miller", "Dutch", "ground grain", "prowled" and "beams dusty with flour", left Noah struggling to comprehend this foreign world. Struggling with the words was an obvious barrier to his understanding, instantly reducing his capacity to visualise and make sense of the culturally unfamiliar scene. Faced with these countless small barriers, he struggled to make sense of the story and its structure.

Crucially, Noah was able to talk with his Dad about the text, checking the meaning of words, asking questions, testing out ideas, thereby mediating the complexity of the story. I was able to nudge his comprehension with questions about the text, prompting him with useful knowledge, creating bridges between the language and the ideas, helping him link up the sentences and meaning across the broader text structure. We could go beyond just word knowledge to tease out his knowledge of similar stories and much more. Such support proved both very useful and likely motivational for Noah.

But we should consider: What gap opens when we set such homework tasks for all of our pupils? What support factors outside the school gate compound the reading gap in the classroom? What classroom talk will bring reading difficult texts to life for our pupils?

I noticed Noah independently applied helpful reading comprehension strategies, like rereading the questions that attended the text and underlining what he deemed important words and phrases. I asked him whether he had been taught to use the underlining strategy, but he claimed it as his own idea. Admittedly, Noah is not always a reliable narrator of his own life, so I took this assertion with a pinch of salt, but his strategic approach to reading was positive and informative nonetheless.

More broadly then, as teachers, we can be intent on making visible these important comprehension strategies, explicitly practising and modelling them to build our comprehension, while attending to developing our pupils' knowledge of the world and of reading conventions. By doing so, we offer additional tools for our pupils to access what they read, particularly when their background knowledge is lacking (which happens in most classrooms!).

Put simply, by better understanding comprehension, and what to do about it in the classroom, our pupils wondering about windmills in a state of confusion can be converted to inspiring wonder about our world as it is explored via reading.

Building 'mental models' of what we read

As we read, we seek to make sense of the content, whether it is a narrative scene set in a windmill, or an informational text about energy in GCSE physics, we seek out a coherent mental model[5] for the text. That is to say, we piece together an image of a scene, or the logical sequence, in an explanation for a scientific process.

How do pupils best build these mental models to understand the world and what they read of it?

A slow, effortful integration of lots of background knowledge matters for all comprehension of course.[6] The more Noah knows about windmills in Holland, the easier it is for him to visualise a narrative scene and understand words like "miller" and "Dutch". Without doubt, this background knowledge matches our knowledge of words, so then vocabulary knowledge proves one useful indicator of reading comprehension.[7]

Noah will also require a good understanding of the conventions of language and stories, such as typical narrative and text structures. So, knowing the conventions of story openings will help him orientate himself as to where the tale of Katje begins and likely ends. Also, grasping the structure of sentences – where the words and ideas connect, within and across sentences – will matter to him building a mental model of the story too. Without doubt, drawing upon a vast breadth of background knowledge as he reads will be of crucial importance.

There are many popular examples to show just how reliant we are on background knowledge to access what we read. Whether it is baseball, or the nuanced art of origami, it is easy to select obscure topics that could baffle even the most experienced of adult readers. And yet, we needn't move very far from the school curriculum to see this occurrence. How about comprehending this sentence from an AQA GCSE physics equations sheet?

> Force on a conductor (at right angles to a magnetic field) carrying a current
>
> = magnetic flux density x current x length.

Like Milton's daughters translating Latin, you may read the words in this sentence with very little meaningful comprehension if you are not a scientist. Unless you grasp the meaning and utility of GCSE physics equations, this passage is near inscrutable.

For older pupils in particular, they face a unique challenge in that they need lots of background knowledge to access academic reading, but of course, this invariably requires lots of reading of texts when you don't yet have the requisite knowledge. It feels like a 'catch-22'.

You could watch a film of a play, or a David Attenborough documentary, to help build your background knowledge before you read a given text, but it still wouldn't give you the necessary knowledge of complex linguistic structures, given the language of written school texts are more complex than film media.[8] To compound the issue, by simplifying language and concepts for our pupils – in an attempt to make the curriculum accessible – such as offering digestible gobbets of information on sleek PowerPoint slides, we limit the practice of reading extended, complex academic texts that is required to become an expert reader.

We cannot simply teach all the background knowledge at the exact right time and in the exact right order. That said, sequencing knowledge in the curriculum with care is a meaningful task.

For Noah, if he had learnt about windmills, perhaps the tale would make more sense and likely offer him a richer mental model to aid comprehension. The limitations of being able to teach every item of knowledge in the right order are obvious given the sheer scale of the task. As a result, every pupil will also need judicious instruction on how to read strategically, so that they can accrue new knowledge when their existing background knowledge is lacking.

We can see in the minutiae of the classroom – like Noah stopping to underline key words and phrases – the value and necessity of being taught to read strategically, while developing his ever-growing store of background knowledge.

The importance of inference making

Consider your knowledge of the following words and idioms (a saying common to a language):

- salary
- worth one's salt
- decimation
- the die is cast
- December

How many ideas and *inferences* – or educated guesses – can you generate from these words and idioms? How would you connect and organise them in relation to one another?

You may have paired 'salary' with 'worth one's salt', given they both relate to money and being worthy of pay or wealth. If you were to dig into the depths of the etymology (the word history) of both you could add layers of inferred knowledge, from the word 'salary' deriving from the Latin '*salarium*' – or wages – given Roman soldiers were often paid money to buy salt, due to how valuable a resource it proved. To be 'worth one's salt' then is more closely bound to our salary than we may have thought.

Equally, we may infer a connection between 'decimation' and 'December' given both include the prefix, from the Latin *decem*, meaning 'ten'. 'December' denoted the tenth month in the Roman calendar. Interestingly, 'decimate' has a rather more gruesome history, as it likely derives from the punishment levelled at mutinous or insubordinate Roman soldiers, with one in ten being killed by lottery as a warning.[9]

We may, if we explore the history of the idiom, 'the die is cast', once more dig into Roman roots. It is said that Julius Caesar uttered this famed saying as he crossed the Rubicon river, in Italy, with his army. Effectively, it connotes a point of no return being reached, with the die being one of a pair of dice that was thrown.

With an in-depth knowledge of each of these words and idioms you can make many more inferences and connections between them. They prove the vital pieces in the jigsaw from which to piece together the big picture of a text in the classroom. In this example, the shared Roman and Latin reference points offer a memorable framework to aid our pupils in developing a rich mental model of what is being read.

Indeed, when we consider the development of a broad, rich curriculum experience for our pupils, we can begin with the building blocks of our reading choices, and on a micro level, the language that builds our pupils' mental model of the world and its history. Teaching 'the Romans' is in part lots of meaningful decisions about what pupils read and what language they develop.

The ability to make multiple inferences from words, phrases and linguistic devices, is one of the factors that mark out successful readers.[10] In the KS2 SATs reading paper, it is made obvious by the marks scheme, with a whopping 70% in the 2018 paper[11] and around half the marks in 2019.[12] We know that pupils who struggle with reading comprehension exhibit a reduced knowledge of idioms and figurative expressions,[13] like metaphors and exaggeration, etc., and so they make fewer inferences from what they read.

E. D. Hirsch puts the challenge of making inferences from what we read plainly and succinctly: "To grasp the words on a page we have to know a lot of information that isn't set down on a page."[14]

Teachers can model inference making in its simplest sense by exploring the layers of meaning in a singular word as we read rich texts. Around 80% of all of the words in English are polysemous:[15] that is to say, they have multiple meanings. And so, generating multiple inferences for given words, phrases, idioms and more, isn't some additional luxury reading skill, but a fundamental aspect of reading successfully in school. Asking questions, making predictions, strategically linking up our background knowledge, all service inference making.

The shifting nature of the language in different subject domains adds a unique layer of challenge for our pupils seeking to make such inferences about what they read in academic texts. For example, in terms of vocabulary, a 'solution' in science is very different to a 'solution' in history; 'bleeding' in art or textiles has a very different meaning to 'bleeding' in a tragedy in English literature. The jigsaw pieces subtly changing shape on our pupils can inhibit their ability to piece together the big picture of reading comprehension.

Inference making then is about *knowing* – a rich combination of background knowledge, word knowledge, genre knowledge and a knowledge of language – and *doing* – activating that knowledge, questioning it, recognising gaps in knowledge and cohering it into a comprehensive whole.

We could continue to invoke and extend the analogy of reading being like the making of a jigsaw. The knowledge of words, genres and the topic are the pieces of the jigsaw. Then there is the active process of piecing together the jigsaw. The term for this monitoring and control we undertake as we think and read is called 'metacognition'.[16] It describes those crucial thought processes we undertake as we read: questioning, building mental models, noticing when we do not understand. Of course, you can't be metacognitive without cognition – without knowledge – otherwise the jigsaw picture remains incomplete, no matter how skilful you are about connecting together pieces.

Pupils who behave more metacognitively – planning their reading, monitoring their understanding as they read, updating what they know and questioning what they do not – are more able to access complex texts and challenging tasks like answering an array of reading comprehension questions.[17]

Teachers can anticipate many of the potential gaps in the jigsaw of our pupils' background knowledge based on their likely age-related experiences (though not all). Our curriculum design can also make a careful attempt to cumulatively and explicitly connect knowledge together in a meaningful sequence. For example, in computing we would teach what 'algorithms' are in KS1 and KS2, before we teach problem solving and 'decomposition' to undertake those complex 'algorithms'. These concepts make more sense connected in a broader mental model of computer science.

Regardless of our best laid lesson plans, we always have to be responsive to supporting pupils' reading and helping them make tentative inferences when their background knowledge is lacking. Alas, it is often the case that we have taught the requisite knowledge already, but our pupils didn't learn it! Not only that, sometimes pupils can 'know' a fact or a word, but they fail to activate it and make the requisite inferences and connect up related words and ideas.

A problem with the reading comprehension of an individual pupil is its sheer unpredictability. It depends upon how much you know and how strategic a reader you are, not just on how much background knowledge you possess.[18] The depth of our pupils' reading comprehension is often only teased out in extended classroom dialogue. Short SATs questions usually tell us too little.

Graham Nuttall, in his seminal research on the 'hidden lives of learners', videoed thousands of hours of learning in the classroom. He found that pupils will likely already know between 40% and 50% of what we teach them.[19] The problem is that they won't all possess the *same* background knowledge. As such, we can never assume the 'full' comprehension of a text from all of our pupils. Therefore, surfacing inference making during reading, such as explicitly questioning the text, or the author in fiction texts, as we read[20] is essential practice in every classroom.

Organising a coherent and cumulative curriculum, with lots of rich reading, and talk about reading, at its heart, is essential in building our pupils' knowledge. Carefully targeted vocabulary teaching can aid the inferencing process and thereby elicit understanding, while we need to encourage our pupils to notice words and their multiple meanings and connections independently (a metacognitive awareness that is helpfully termed 'word consciousness'). Questioning and talk, to draw out what pupils know and understand of what they read, is imperative. Getting pupils to write about their reading,[21] to elaborate and reflect on their thinking and to update their predictions, will help too.

It is important to teach, model and guide inference making as we read,[22] such as asking precise questions or discussing layers of meaning in a text in classroom dialogue, so it is helpful for every teacher to know the different types of inferences we generate as we read strategically.

The following table shows a selection of inference types to help navigate our way through reading a text.[23]

To make this more concrete, grab the last thing that you read (on your phone, bookshelf, etc.) and then retrospectively consider where and what inferences you made from just a single paragraph of that text. You can label the different types of inference L, G, C, El, P and Ev. What becomes clear is that all reading is highly active – like our eye movements being constantly on the move – and we are constantly seeking coherence and building a mental model of the text.

Reading is no passive, static act of merely receiving information. What the author conveys in the text matters, but just as crucial to what is read and understood relates to what the reader brings to the text. Good readers are meaning makers, not passive recipients.

For every teacher, this process is largely intuitive and tacit, done quickly and expertly. However, if we were to foreground the thinking of an expert reader more explicitly, making visible the important knowledge not set down on the page, we can better guide our pupils to read successfully.

When teachers know the different inference types more specifically, we can better target our questioning to both model and encourage reading comprehension. We can also better develop a coherent and cumulative curriculum that

Inference type	Definition	Example
Local inferences (L)	The making of coherent links between and across sentences and paragraphs. Sometimes the ties between sentences are made explicit, whereas at others they remain implicit. In the example, the reader would recognise how fairy tales are invoked, but then how Dahl playfully rejects that genre reference	"In fairy tales, witches always wear silly black hats and black coats, and they ride on broomsticks. But this is not a fairy tale." *Witches*, by Roald Dahl, p. 1
Global inferences (G)	The making of broader links between the main theme or point of a text across the whole text. In the example, the reader would synthesise how the life of Darwin transcended a typical life and proved seminal for science	A biography of Charles Darwin that focuses on his theory of natural selection and his vital importance to the field of biology

Inference type	Definition	Example
Cohesive inferences (C)	'Filling the gaps' and maintaining coherence between sentences, such as noting the vocabulary that acts as 'cohesive ties' and bridges between sentences (akin to local inferences). In the example, the reader would compare and contrast the qualities of paper in both sentences, with 'although' cohering both sentences	'Paper is a cheap and lightweight material. Although it is sensitive to moisture and is not a robust material.'
Elaborative inferences (EI)	The enriching additions we bring to the text to add meaning and greater coherence. In the example, the reader would draw upon their political and historical knowledge to judge America	"America was never innocent." *American Tabloid*, by James Ellroy, p. 4

(continued)

Inference type	Definition	Example
Predictive inferences (P)	The ability to look forward in a text and make appropriate predictions. In this (famous) example, the reader would assume that something perfect – indeed supernatural – may attend the Dursleys, or other inhabitants of "four Privet Drive"	"Mr and Mrs Dursley, of number four Privet Drive, were proud to say that they were perfectly normal, thank you very much." *Harry Potter and the Philosopher's Stone*, by J. K. Rowling, p. 1
Evaluative inferences (Ev)	The ability to look back in a text and draw conclusions and evaluate. In the example, pupils would likely, without prompting, organise their understanding of Hinduism by evaluating it in comparison with other religions they know	After reading about Hinduism in religious education, pupils may evaluate and compare it with their knowledge of the Christian and Muslim faiths

connects the jigsaw pieces together, anticipating our best laid plans will fail, so we can nurture reading strategies and repair gaps in comprehension.

It is helpful to consider when such inferences are typically being made *before, during* or *after* the act of reading. *Predictive inferences* often occur before reading a text (though we update these predictions continually), whereas *cohesive* and *elaborative inferences* typically happen during reading, with *evaluative inferences* commonly occurring after we have read the text. Though simplistic, this is a helpful lens through which to consider our teaching of reading.

We ask questions of the text we read in class all the time without recourse to any fancy labels regarding inference making. And yet, with greater precision about the questions asked in the classroom during reading, alongside the knowledge we expect our pupils to draw upon, we can ensure that our pupils better comprehend school texts with success.

Take these opening paragraphs from the 2017 KS2 reading test, labelled 'Swimming the English Channel':

On a foggy August afternoon in 1875, a lone swimmer dived from Admiralty Pier in Dover into the cold waters of the English Channel. Nearly twenty-two hours later, the exhausted man staggered onto French soil at Calais and became an instant hero. Captain Matthew Webb had become the first person to swim across the English Channel.

Twenty-seven-year-old Webb was a merchant seaman from Shropshire. He had always been a powerful swimmer and, hearing of J.B. Thompson's failed attempt to swim the Channel in 1872, he was inspired to give up his job and train as a long-distance swimmer. Webb's first attempt had to be abandoned due to bad weather, but he returned to the icy Channel water two weeks later.

We make local inferences speedily during the act of reading – such as assuming the "lone swimmer" from the opening sentence is the "exhausted man" from the following sentence. The text holds back the name of the man until the end of the opening paragraph (perhaps for dramatic effect?). For some pupils, they are working very hard to cohere the scene and place the journey from Dover to Calais, so they will be strained to make all the necessary connections *and* then go on to offer cogent answers to comprehension questions.

In the comprehension test questions, pupils have to retrieve words that connote the Captain being tired and to state what inspired his heroic feat. Many more questions and inferences are triggered in the minds of our pupils for them to cohere a full mental model of the text, such as:

- Who is the "lone swimmer" in the opening sentence? [L/C]
- What do we know about the challenge of crossing the Channel? [G/El]
- What do you think was Captain's Webb's inspiration? [El/Ev]

Each layer of comprehension sees us seek out specific information, but also actively predict and elaborate upon what is being read. Such questions, modelled by the teacher, posed to pupils, discussed and debated, offer the essence of successful strategic reading instruction. We connect the words on the page with what E. D. Hirsch described as the "information that isn't set down on the page" by reading, listening, talking, questioning and building our models of the text and the world.[24]

Our emotional and psychological response to reading a text of course matters. This 'reader response' to real-life characters like Captain Webb is subtly mingled with what we know about geography, history and our English weather, in building a rich mental model and understanding what we read. It is a bridge to understanding what happens every day in almost every classroom.

Many of the pupils we teach will require lots of our attentive guidance and support to cross such bridges. If they do not bridge that gap, they won't learn. If our pupils reach their teens without crossing these bridges, the job becomes harder for both them and their teachers.[25]

Every teacher worth their salt then should be intent on ensuring every pupil becomes a knowledgeable and strategic reader.

Building bridges and burying the dead

First, let's begin with a simple reading passage, followed by a question:

> There was a tourist flight from Vienna to Barcelona. On the last leg of the journey, it developed engine trouble. Over the Pyrenees, the pilot started to lose control. The plane eventually crashed right on the border. Wreckage was equally strewn in France and Spain. The authorities were trying to decide where to bury the survivors.
> 'A Case Study of Anomaly Detection: Shallow Semantic Processing and Cohesion Establishment', by S. B. Barton & A. J. Sandford, p. 479[26]

The simple question: *Where should the authorities bury the survivors?*

Where did you plump for: France or Spain? Perhaps you slowed your thinking down a little and made a more considered response? Read the final sentence again: How can a *survivor* be buried anywhere? We bury the dead!

This question is based on research from Barton and Sandford on the reading glitches we are all prone to – or 'anomaly detection'[27] – as they term it. Once more, they show how our reading and thinking can be flawed and prone to damaging gaps and mistakes.

Akin to the 'Moses illusion' from Chapter 3, it reveals how even expert adult readers can fail to accurately comprehend everything we read. It isn't just a gimmicky piece of fun – it is indicative of how reading comprehension requires careful, effortful attention to what is being read, so that we can build a complete mental model of the text at hand.

It is also indicative of that classic teacher experience when you are convinced you taught X brilliantly on Monday, but by Thursday it is as if X was never taught, nor existed in the minds of our pupils!

Remember the description of my own novice reader grappling with *Katje the Windmill Cat*? You may recall how I described him underlining important words and phrases in the text to effectively track his thinking. It is strategic actions like this, part of being metacognitive – thinking about our thinking – that we term more specifically 'comprehension monitoring'. This accurately describes the careful, deliberate way we read when we are seeking out understanding and noticing when we do not know or understand. When a pupil gets stuck reading a science textbook, and notices that fact, they are comprehension monitoring.

Now, we are always comprehension monitoring as we read. You are doing it right now. Effectively, it is the constant checking process a skilled reader undertakes – though it is usually done tacitly and without much conscious awareness. The 'bury the survivors' example jars so much because it makes this awareness explicit to you.

For a pupil, they could read a simple sentence like 'the cat leapt on the mat' with relative ease. But then, if we replace a word, such as 'the *vase* leapt on the mat', pupils may trigger their comprehension monitoring into action and think 'that isn't quite right'. Now, if the text was a fairy tale, such as 'Beauty and the Beast', they could infer from their knowledge of the genre that this is instead a plausible, apt description.

This comprehension-monitoring process reveals how active reading is as a process. We are always cross-referencing the words, ideas, structures and language from a text with our existing knowledge, updating and evaluating our mental model along the way.[28]

Comprehension monitoring can exist at a 'local' level or a 'global' level. So, we could make evaluative inferences about the global structure of a text. Take this familiar fairy-tale sequence – from 'The Three Little Pigs' – and monitor whether any of the text details violate our sense of time order – that is to say, our knowledge of the global structure of the text:

- Three little pigs leave their home to seek adventure in the world.
- The three little pigs find a plot to build a new home.
- One pig builds a house of straw, another a house of sticks, another a house of bricks.
- A wolf came along, blew down the house of bricks and ate the little pig.
- The wolf then blew down the house of sticks and ate the little pig.
- The wolf couldn't blow down the house of straw, so he climbed down the chimney.
- The pig set a pot of water boiling and when the wolf fell in, so the pig closed the lid and cooked the wolf.
- The little pig lived happily ever after.

Reading comprehension

What subtle shift in the fairy-tale structure did you note was out of place? Of course, the house of bricks is never blown down. Such structural details often rely on a reader's background knowledge of the story, alongside typical generic patterns and structures. Now, with this task you had a precise goal to note the narrative structure of the tale. This explicit goal helps our comprehension – effectively shrinking the problem – like a teacher directing pupils to monitor the structure of the text, or to make a local inference about a word or a phrase.

Although pupils' reading habitually is a vital source for them to learn new words, there is evidence to show that pupils may gain an understanding of less than 15% of the unknown vocabulary items in the texts they read.[29] As we grapple to make sense of a text, small details can be lost. Pupils can struggle to gain the meaning of words from the surrounding text.[30] Their comprehension monitoring therefore fails.

It is important then to explicitly teach, model and scaffold comprehension monitoring and inference making. This is the heart of teaching reading. We can model those crucial comprehension monitoring 'reduce/repair strategies'. These are the strategies a good reader undertakes to repair miscomprehensions e.g.

- skimming (reading rapidly for a general overview of the text);
- scanning (reading rapidly to find specific information);
- slowing down;
- rereading;
- reading back through the text;
- checking the index, glossary or scaffolds;
- asking questions;
- summarising;

- noticing patterns and text structures; and
- reading related texts.[31]

They seem obvious to us, but we are expert readers – not novices juggling and struggling with an array of new information.

Take a moment to consider:

- How deliberately do you chunk down the act of reading, so that pupils grasp the before, during and after of a skilled reader?
- How consistently do you model and highlight comprehension monitoring (e.g. by asking questions to prompt understanding, by modelling rereading or looking back in the text for information)?
- How often do you assume a text that has been read has been understood?

Let's pursue these questions further. Figure 4.1 includes some prompts to consider what a strategic reader may do as they actively monitor what they read.

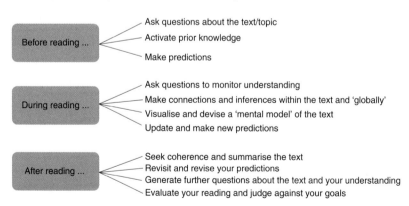

Figure 4.1   Reading: before, during and after

Adapted from Cameron, S. (2009) *Teaching reading comprehension strategies*. New Zealand: Pearson, p. 11.

Reading comprehension

As we unpick the steps taken by an expert reader at each stage of the reading process to secure their comprehension, we can be more explicit about modelling these steps for, and with, our pupils. From the micro details of making inferences and monitoring comprehension, we can also break down the macro process of reading to learn.

Such deliberate approaches to reading can be applied and adapted in the year 1 classroom as much as in the A level science classroom. The effort exerted in such academic reading ultimately pays off in school success – so that we don't have to bother with the wasted effort of burying survivors!

Reading with a role and a goal

> Some books are to be tasted, others to be swallowed and some few to be chewed and digested.
>
> 'Of Studies', by Francis Bacon[32]

Back in 1627, Francis Bacon made the sage observation that not all reading is equal. On any given day we could go from reading a shopping list, to a webpage on the news of the day, then on to a classic novel.

For each act of reading we will have different goals, allocate different degrees of our attention and even play different roles. How we usually expect our pupils to read in class is an effortful and attentive reading of the text – properly chewed and digested – and unlike much of their reading outside of the school gates.

Pupils are expected to deliberate, record, remember and connect what they read countless times a day. It proves a complex, tiring, but ultimately rewarding process. We may expect the deep comprehension of a complex text, but at other times we direct them to skim and scan for key information – a mere taste. Being explicit about the different goals for reading, and the best strategies to get there, can too often remain implicit to weaker readers.

The specificity of the goal of our reading matters to what we remember. An elegant reading experiment from the 1970s showed how reading with specific goals and roles in mind actually alters what we remember.[33] Readers were given a passage about two boys playing truant from school and going to one of their homes. Crucially though, the readers were given the role of either a 'home buyer' or a 'burglar' before their first reading of the text. Unsurprisingly, this role affected what was remembered from the actual text. Burglars remembered a little more, but both groups remembered different details. Reading details about open doors matter to burglars in different ways to homeowners. When the students were asked to flip the roles for a second reading of the text, the readers suppressed the former role and remembered more of what was salient to their new perspective.

So how does this relate to school? We are certainly not aiming for a school full of highly accomplished thieves. We should however consider how carefully framing our instructions for reading with specific goals, and sometimes different roles, will help both recall of what is read, but also deepen understanding.

For young pupils, perhaps reading a text about Viking history, we may encourage them to take on the character of an archaeologist, digging beneath the surface of the text/s to unveil insights of historical value and to categorise and record. For pupils in secondary school, we can fully characterise a historian and how they piece together the jigsaw of historical chronology in narratives and lines of enquiry. We should be explicit in defining how a historian works: their criticality, how they carefully distinguish a source and tease out a narrative from the Viking fragments, alongside secondary sources, with a degree of due tentativeness and more.

An example of the importance of allocating reading goals and roles was highlighted to me at a training event last year, when a primary school colleague approached me with an anecdote from his classroom. He had recently invested in copies of *Young Sherlock Holmes* for his class. Quickly, he realised the language was too challenging for many of his pupils. In response, he borrowed the notion of 'reading detectives' and effectively gave his pupils a role that would foreground comprehension monitoring as they read the story, selecting difficult words and important information. Happily, the struggle of reading a highly complex text was now pitched as an intriguing challenge. Pupils would record interesting vocabulary and track the plot more attentively and deliberately.

Whether it is reading detectives exploring *Sherlock Holmes*, a historian reading a fragment of a biography of Shakespeare or a Germanist translating a difficult *BILD* newspaper article, having a clear goal and role focuses attention and this can aid the pursuit of comprehension.

Another approach to allocating roles to make reading a more strategic act is the 'reciprocal-reading' approach. Coined by Palinscar and Brown in 1984,[34] reciprocal reading is a collaborative approach to reading. Pupils are trained, with explicit modelling by the teacher, to take on the role of *predictor, questioner, clarifier* and *summariser* (see Figure 4.2).

The effectiveness of reciprocal reading[35] likely derives from the allocation of roles that makes the strategic aspect of reading explicit and clear. It makes comprehension monitoring visible to every pupil, while it can draw upon

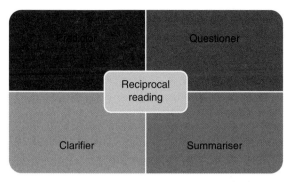

Figure 4.2   Reciprocal reading

their collective background knowledge. There is the potential danger of collective miscomprehensions, or simply being distracted by peers, but if the reciprocal reading method is closely guided by the teacher, it can have powerful benefits. When undertaken in small groups with pupils identified as struggling readers, it can prove most effective.[36]

If we return to the 'Swimming the English Channel' passage and Captain Webb, we can consider how we prime pupils' understanding before they read. We can *question* the character of an army captain by way of *predicting* his character; we can *clarify* the geography, and challenge, of crossing the Channel; we can *summarise* attitudes to Webb after conquering the mammoth challenge, etc. In doing so, we aid pupils to infer, activate their prior knowledge and repeatedly check and cohere their comprehension. In short, we model the act of expert reading.

And so, we come to summarise this chapter on comprehension.

Have you cohered a useful mental model for how pupils best comprehend what they read? Did you achieve your reading goals as a teacher? For pupils in every classroom, these questions shouldn't be left to chance.

IN SHORT ...

- Reading comprehension is the goal of all reading, but it is complex to decipher, and we can only 'observe indirect symptoms' of it in the classroom. We *can* recognise the vast store of knowledge and skill that is deployed as we seek to cohere meaning and teach reading more explicitly.
- Each time we read we seek out a 'mental model' of the whole text. That is to say, we make many connections and inferences, seeking to organise them into a coherent whole. We can make inferences – educated guesses and links to our background knowledge – on a 'local' level, linking words and sentences together, alongside 'global' inferences, which make links across whole texts and beyond.
- A strategic approach to making inferences, questioning a text and building a mental model is termed 'comprehension monitoring'. This active, strategic approach can be modelled and taught explicitly with the allocation of reading comprehension goals and roles in the classroom.
- Teaching approaches like 'reciprocal reading', and similar, offer a structure to explicitly teach comprehension monitoring and for pupils to deliberately practise reading-comprehension strategies.

Notes

1 Law, J., Charlton, J., Dockrell, J., Gascoigne, M., McKean, C., & Theakston, A. (2017). *Early language development: Needs, provision, and intervention for pre-school children from socioeconomically disadvantaged backgrounds.* Newcastle

University review for the Education Endowment Foundation. London: Education Endowment Foundation.

2 Gough, P. B., Hoover, W. A., & Peterson, C. L. (1996). Some observations on a simple view of reading. In C. Cornoldi & J. V. Oakhill (Eds.), *Reading comprehension difficulties: Processes and interventions* (pp. 1–13). Mahwah, NJ: Lawrence Erlbaum Associates.

3 Pearson, P. D., & Hamm, D. N. (2005). The assessment of reading comprehension: A review of practices – past, present, and future. In S. G. Paris & S. A. Stahl (Eds.), *Children's reading comprehension and assessment* (pp. 13–69). Mahwah, NJ, US: Lawrence Erlbaum Associates.

4 Woelfle, G., *Katje the windmill cat*. London: Walker Books, p. 3.

5 Glenberg, A. M., Meyer, M., & Lindem, K. (1987). Mental models contribute to foregrounding during text comprehension. *Journal of Memory and Language, 26*(1), 69–83.

6 Willingham, D. (2006). How knowledge helps. *American Educator*. Retrieved from www.aft.org/periodical/american-educator/spring-2006/how-knowledge-helps.

7 Spencer, M., Wagner, R. K., & Petscher, Y. (2019). The reading comprehension and vocabulary knowledge of children with poor reading comprehension despite adequate decoding: Evidence from a regression-based matching approach. *Journal of Educational Psychology, 111*(1), 1–14. http://dx.doi.org/10.1037/edu0000274.

8 Baines, L. (1996). From page to screen: When a novel is interpreted for film, what gets lost in the translation? *Journal of Adolescent & Adult Literacy, 39*(8), 612–622.

9 The etymology of 'decimation' is not without debate. See this web article from the *Oxford Dictionary*, retrieved from https://blog.oxforddictionaries.com/2012/09/10/does-decimate-mean-destroy-one-tenth.

10 Cain, K., & Oakhill, J. V. (1999). Inference making and its relation to comprehension failure. *Reading and Writing, 11*, 489–503.

11 Clarke, R. (2018). The 2018 KS2 reading SATs: Expert analysis. Retrieved from https://freedomtoteach.collins.co.uk/the-2018-ks2-reading-sats-expert-analysis.

12 Department for Education (2019). *2019 key stage 2 English reading test mark schemes Reading answer booklet*. Retrieved from https://assets.publishing.service.gov.uk/government/uploads/system/uploads/attachment_data/file/803889/STA198212e_2019_ks2_English_reading_Mark_schemes.pdf.

13 Cain, K., & Towse, A. S. (2008). To get hold of the wrong end of the stick: Reasons for poor idiom understanding in children with reading comprehension difficulties. *Journal of Speech, Language, and Hearing Research, 51*(6), 1538–1549. https://doi.org/10.1044/1092-4388(2008/07-0269).

14 Hirsch, E. D. (1994). *Cultural literacy: What every American needs to know*. Boulder, CO: Westview Press, p. 3.

15 Rodd, J. (2017). Lexical ambiguity. In M. G. Gaskell & S. A. Rueschemeyer (Eds.), *Oxford handbook of psycholinguistics*. Oxford: Oxford University Press. Retrieved from https://psyarxiv.com/yezc6.

16 Education Endowment Foundation (2018). *Metacognition and self-regulation*. London: Education Endowment Foundation.

17 Ibid.

18 Cain, K., Oakhill, J. V., Barnes, M. A., & Bryant, P. E. (2001). Comprehension skill, inference-making ability, and their relation to knowledge. *Memory & Cognition, 29*, 850–859.

19 Nutthall, G. (2007). *The hidden lives of learners*. Wellington, NZ: NZCER Press.

20 Oakhill, J. V., Cain, K., & Elbro, K. (2014). *Understanding reading comprehension: A handbook*. Oxford: Routledge; Beck, I., & McKeown, M. (2002). Questioning the author: Making sense of social studies. *Reading and Writing in the Content Areas, 60*(3), 44–47.

21 Graham, S., & Hebert, M. A. (2010). *Writing to read: Evidence for how writing can improve reading. A Carnegie Corporation time to act report*. Washington, DC: Alliance for Excellent Education.

22 Elleman, A. (2017). Examining the impact of inference instruction on the literal and inferential comprehension of skilled and less skilled readers: A meta-analytic review. *Journal of Educational Psychology, 109*(6), 761–781.

23 Kispal, A. (2008). Effective teaching of inference skills for reading: Literature review. Retrieved from www.nfer.ac.uk/publications/EDR01/EDR01.pdf.

24 Hirsch, E. D. (1994). *Cultural literacy: What every American needs to know.* Boulder, CO: Westview Press, p. 3.

25 Davis, M. H., McPartland, J. M., Pryseski, C., & Kim, E. (2018). The effects of coaching on English teachers' reading instruction practices and adolescent students' reading comprehension. *Literacy Research and Instruction, 57*(3), 255–275. doi:10.1080/19388071.2018.1453897.

26 Barton, S. B., & Sanford, A. J. (1993). A case study of anomaly detection: Shallow semantic processing and cohesion establishment. *Memory and Cognition, 21*(4), 477–487.

27 Ibid.

28 Van der Schoot, M., Reijntjes, A., & van Lieshout, E. C. D. M. (2012). How do children deal with inconsistencies in text? An eye fixation and self-paced reading study in good and poor reading comprehenders. *Reading and Writing, 25*(7), 1665–1690. doi:10.1007/s11145-011-9337-4.

29 De Glopper, K., & Swanborn, M. S. L. (1999). Incidental word learning while reading: A meta-analysis. *Review of Educational Research, 69*(3), 261–285. https://doi.org/(...)02/00346543069003261.

30 Cain, K., & Oakhill, J. V. (2007). Reading comprehension difficulties: Correlates, causes and consequences. In K. Cain & J. V. Oakhill (Eds.), *Children's comprehension problems in oral and written language* (pp. 41–75). New York, NY: Guilford Press.

31 Amzil, A. (2014). The effect of a metacognitive intervention on college students' reading performance and metacognitive skills. *Journal of Educational and Developmental Psychology, 4*(1), 27–45.

32 Bacon, F. (n.d.). 'Of studies'. In *Essays of Francis Bacon.* Retrieved from www.authorama.com/essays-of-francis-bacon-50.html.

33 Pichert, J. W., & Anderson, R. C. (1977). Taking different perspectives on a story. *Journal of Educational Psychology, 69*(4), 309–315. http://dx.doi.org/10.1037/0022-0663.69.4.309.

34 Palincsar, A., & Brown, A. L. (1984). Reciprocal teaching of comprehension-fostering and monitoring activities. *Cognition and Instruction, 1*(2), 117–175.

35 Education Endowment Foundation (2019). *Reciprocal reading.* Retrieved from https://education endowment foundation.org.uk/pdf/generate/?u=https://education endowmentfoundation.org.uk/pdf/project/?id=956&t= EEF%20Projects&e=956&s=.

36 Ibid.

5 Reading barriers

Some moments in teaching leave a lasting impression upon you like the rings within an oak tree. When deciding upon whether I would become a teacher, while in my last year of university, I spent a week in a local special school. In a single day, I hurtled from shearing sheep on the school farm, painting in art, to a traditional maths lesson.

The experience that endures most for me from the first day of that week – even more so than grappling with the sheep on the farm – was reading with Matthew. This young man was in his late teens, but as a reader he was more like a child over ten years his junior. As his parents took a tour of the special school, I was asked to read with him. Unfettered by knowing how to actually teach, I sat alongside him and listened to him read.

Remembering how Matthew read, slowly and earnestly, tripping over words in every sentence, is still vivid in my mind nearly two decades on. In truth, I was frightened by just how little I knew about supporting him to read. It would become a familiar feeling teaching many of my pupils throughout my teaching career. Instinctively, I would support Matthew by cueing letter sounds for him, sometimes offering whole words and phrases to keep him reading.

Reading each page with Matthew proved a small victory.

I recall Matthew being incredulous that the protagonist of this early reading tale planned on leaving home and his parents. It revealed to me with a tender shock how our comprehension can be bounded by the limits of our experience. The actions of the character were incomprehensible to Matthew in every way: both cognitively and emotionally.

Despite the plodding pace, Matthew eventually reached the end of the short book. As he did so, he shouted with surprised delight.

Though I'd read countless times in my life, perhaps no other experience brought home the power of reading like that snatched 20 minutes before lunchtime reading with Matthew. I'd taken for granted the joy that could accompany reading achievement.

I made a determined, private commitment to myself that day to become a teacher and to learn how to teach pupils to read to the best of my ability. I would no longer take the simple, but profound pleasure and power of reading for granted.

Every once in a while, I wonder whether Matthew has now left home, if he can now read fluently and whether he possesses books he can call his own.

For Matthew, and every other pupil in our care, it is clearly essential that we best support their reading in school and better diagnose potential reading challenges and difficulties so that we can do something about it.

Why *Mr Men* books may be more difficult than you think

Most teachers can identify pupils like Matthew who struggle with reading, but too few teachers are confident about what to do about it. An important starting point is understanding what determines the intrinsic difficulty of what we read in classrooms.

Every year, media headlines abound about the difficulty of children's books. This BBC headline neatly captures the running theme: *"Mr Greedy* 'almost as hard to read' as Steinbeck classics."[1] In response, incredulous commentators claim such evidence is devised by 'Mr Nonsense in Nonsenseland'. They have a point. Renaissance UK, who undertake large-scale research on around 33,000 children's books, have some useful insights. Their complexity formula is based on calculations related to average word length, word difficulty and sentence length. Now, these readability measures can offer some useful guidance regarding text choices, but they are without doubt flawed too.

Reading complexity comes down to more than simply the number of complex words. If this were the case, *Diary of a Wimpy Kid* – coming in at 20,445 words – could potentially come close to Charles Dicken's novella *A Christmas Carol*, which only comes in at a paltry 16,000 words. It is such calculations that place *Mr Men* tales with a higher difficulty score than Dahl's *Fantastic Mr Fox*. The mature themes and ambiguous characters of Dahl are not accounted for by the calculation.

The relative reading difficulty of a text is related to numerous potential factors. The non-chronological structure of *A Christmas Carol*, and the snakingly long sentences of Dickens, with multiple clauses, mean that it is strikingly difficult for a modern young audience to follow and comprehend. This difficulty is in part mediated by background knowledge. Given most children are familiar with the character of Scrooge (though not many other aspects of Dickensian Britain). The familiar characters of such classic tales, along with archetypal story structures, mean that fiction can often prove easier to access and comprehend than informational texts.[2]

Most academic texts in secondary schools are informational texts, such as science reports, textbook chapters in modern foreign languages and computer science instructions, etc. They are stripped of the emotional associations we can generate from stories and they simply require more background knowledge[3] given they have more rare vocabulary and their concepts are typically separated from everyday life. To compound the issue further, the structure of such informational texts are typically less familiar to our weaker readers.

How crucial then are the length of sentences if they appear commonly in readability formulas? The aforementioned Dickensian sentences no doubt pose added difficulty for our young readers. A long, complex sentence can max out the 'working memory' of our pupils. Our working memory is our short-term capacity to hold multiple items of information in our mind at any one time. Let's make a straightforward comparison of a relatively lengthy sentence that is subtly reordered to increase the challenge on our pupils' working memory:

> Janey looked out from her porch on a sunny and sizzling hot day in August, letting out a smile from ear to ear.

Now, try reading this subtle variation of the same sentence:

> On a sunny and sizzling hot day in August, letting out a smile from ear to ear, Janey looked out from her porch.

Did you notice the subtle difference made by the main subject of the sentence, Janey, and the main verb "looked", being embedded within the middle of the sentence instead of at the beginning?

The multiple clauses arranged in this way simply get our minds working that little bit harder, hunting down the main subject of the sentence.[4] Conversely, you may have read both sentences and found the punctuation that demarcated parts of the sentence in the second example helped its readability. Such a sound understanding of syntax – the structure of sentences – is clearly important to comprehension[5] (though it is not usually as vital as background knowledge and vocabulary knowledge of the content being read).

Remember the GCSE Islam text in Chapter 1, with each sentence being logically connected and syntax mattering a great deal to shaping meaning?

The most common units of sentence structures can be described thus:

- **Word**: teacher
- **Phrase**: the teacher
- **Clause**: the tired teacher
- **Simple sentence**: the tired teacher began reading
- **Complex sentence**: when the bell rang, the teacher began reading
- **Compound sentence**: the bell rang and the teacher quickly began reading

These basic units of language and sentences offer us the building blocks for the text we expect our pupils to read. The more complex the variation, the more barriers it will pose to our novice readers. A very simple proxy for every teacher determining text complexity is to be aware that when a sentence has three or more clauses it is likely to offer an increased degree of challenge to most of our pupils.

Reading barriers

Young children quickly develop an awareness of the typical sentence structures they read. The most common sentence structure is 'subject – verb – object' (SVO). An example would be 'Alex writes books'. You can elaborate on this but actually the SVO structure remains intrinsic to the sentence structure, e.g.

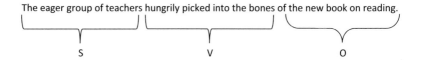

When you add in multiple clauses, with punctuation separating out ideas, pupils are forced into a mental juggling act. At any one time, they are activating their background knowledge, decoding sounds into words, identifying vocabulary and navigating the syntax and whole text structures.

Is it any wonder the complex act of reading is a struggle for so many?

The complexity of syntax is such that exam boards are conscious of not adding unnecessary difficulty to their examination questions. The 'accessibility' list from exam boards regarding their language use for GCSE exams is an excellent example of both how we can mediate reading barriers, but also understand what makes texts difficult. They work to principles such as:

- Put command words at the beginning of the sentence and use one per sentence.
- Add scaffolding to questions to act as a guide (appropriate to level of demand).
- Ensure each sentence contains fewer than 20 words.
- Use bullet points to clearly display specific strands of information.

- Embolden key bits of information.
- Explain unfamiliar terms.
- Include plenty of white space to improve readability.

Adapted from 'Our Exams Explained: GCSE Science
Exams from Summer 2018', by AQA[6]

Many teachers are surprised when they learn that GCSE science exam papers have a reading age of around 13.[7] To put this into context: If they were to place GCSE exams in science at the chronological age of 16, only around half of pupils would comprehend the questions. It would prove more a test of reading than a valid science test.[8]

Exam boards, especially in subjects like science, cannot reduce the intrinsic difficulty of the scientific language – the words and phrases – or the concepts and knowledge required to understand them, so they have to reduce sentence length and complexity. Other minor grammatical features can either make reading more accessible or trickier for pupils. In a science text, adding in an extra clause could well strain our pupils' understanding; however, in some cases, it instead proves helpful and reduces the degree of challenge.

For example:

> Magnesium, **an alkaline earth metal**, is used to make strong, lightweight alloys and it is used in pyrotechnic displays because it burns with a bright light.

Here, the classification of magnesium, helps pupils recognise what group of elements it is part of in the periodic table. The technical term for this added description of a noun is an 'appositive' and it is very common in informational texts in school. And so, it is sometimes the case that an extra embedded clause in a sentence can be helpful for the reader.

Reading barriers

For teachers in year 2 or year 12, having some grasp of the grammatical features of what is being read is helpful, so that teachers can name them and explicitly instruct their pupils to recognise them as they build their mental model of the text being read.

Even reading the *Mr Men* series may require more teacher knowledge than we first assume.

Understanding reading difficulty and the 'arduous eight'

When we explore what makes a school text difficult, we come to explore a whole range of complex, interacting factors. We could best simplify them as the 'arduous eight':

1. Background knowledge – the sheer range of necessary knowledge and related ideas in a given passage or whole text.
2. Range and complexity of vocabulary (including word length).
3. Use of abstract imagery and metaphorical language.
4. Sentence length and syntax.
5. Narrative or whole-text structures.
6. The generic elements of the text, e.g. a biographical account in history.
7. The scaffolds present, or absent, in a given text, e.g. keyword glossary.
8. Text length.

The degree of difficulty is of course always mediated by what the pupil knows and their past reading experience. A lengthy biography of Lionel Messi, complete with images, statistics and football jargon may prove burdensome to a skilled reader who has little knowledge or interest in football. A younger, average reader who is an ardent football fan, may face far fewer reading comprehension difficulties. The reality, though, is that many school topics stand a step removed from our pupils' background knowledge.

There are a range of readability formulas freely available on the Internet, such as the 'Flesch Reading Ease formula', the 'Fog Scale', the 'SMOG Index', etc. to decipher broad notions of the difficulty level of texts. They all, however, have failings and there is not an exact science. Only Mr Nonsense would argue that we have all the answers. Teacher judgement is therefore paramount. Sentence lengths may be accessible, but the ideas in a text may be too mature; the vocabulary of a text may be accessible, but the overall text structure is non-chronological (out of time order) and very difficult to follow.

A really handy approach for teachers to use is Wayne Tennant's 'ready reckoner'.[9] He poses a more accessible 'formula' approach that a busy teacher can wisely apply on a regular basis, while adapting the criteria to their ends too (we could devise a ready reckoner for reading in different subject disciplines, e.g. reading science texts). First, consider the span of readers in the class. Then test the text – fiction book, magazine article, web page, or worksheet, etc. – against the following tripartite criteria (or one based on similar principles):

1. **Difficult words**: Are there tricky words you expect many of the class will struggle to decode or comprehend (with young children, word-reading ability would be the primary consideration, but with older pupils comprehending the words becomes the key marker)?
2. **Language features**: Are there unique metaphors or imagery, complex sentence structures comprising multiple clauses, alongside rarer items of punctuation, e.g. colon usage?

3. **Concepts**: How many different ideas and concepts are evoked by the text? This interacts with 'difficult words', given such unfamiliar vocabulary often introduces a new concept in the classroom.

Now, you could view a 100-word extract from a given text with this 'ready reckoner' lens. If a numerical value is helpful, then start by adding points for each difficult word, language feature and concept in the sample text, then take the 100 number as a starting value and subtract the difficulty number you have collated.

For example, analysing a sample from an online BBC article about climate change may gain the following difficulty score:

1. Difficult words   = 3 points
2. Language features   = 4 points
3. Concepts   = 2 points
    Overall points score = 9 points

Tennant proposes that there can be a rough readability level calculated. Given the 100 starting point:

- 95–100 points = The text is not difficult to comprehend.
- 90–95 points = The text offers an appropriate degree of challenge.
- Less than 90 points = The text may be difficult for some pupils to read independently.

By this reckoning, the BBC climate-change article would have a score of 91 (100 minus 9), which puts it in the range of 'appropriate degree of challenge'. It would therefore prove readable and most pupils could likely access it independently. At other times, a difficult text is desirable, but it would simply require more teacher instruction.

Understanding the elements of language knowledge and background knowledge that make reading a specific text difficult should be an integral part of every teacher's armoury. A coherent reading curriculum in every phase and subject will no doubt help, but a ready reckoner is useful when choices are being made quickly about reading material in class and for homework. A readability score may never quite encompass the actual difficulty of a text – especially if we consider the wealth of different starting points for individuals in a class – but it nevertheless proves useable knowledge for assigning, or supporting, reading in the classroom and beyond.

Finally, an important insight for teachers is the knowledge that many pupils are simply not strategic readers in the face of such barriers. When faced with difficult words or complex sentence structures, they may not bring enough awareness about how to tackle barriers to their understanding.

A cruel truth is that weak readers often don't know what they don't know.

A consensus in the research evidence states that weak readers don't think they should be monitoring their understanding, nor adopting reduce/repair strategies when they face a difficult word or concept.[10] And so, an apt solution is to make the 'arduous eight' visible to every pupil and to explicitly teach them to be strategic in the face of specific reading barriers.

What should every teacher know about dyslexia?

'Dys' = difficult/abnormal; 'lexia' = words

Dyslexia is an emotive subject and for many teachers it evokes a mix of fear and some confusion. Every teacher can recognise the crippling damage wrought by struggling to learn to read, but, as a label, dyslexia is too often a mystery to many teachers. When faced with a pupil with dyslexia – with minimal understanding of literacy barriers proving typical – a natural reaction from teachers is an expectation that the issue will be addressed elsewhere by colleagues with more expertise.

For a pupil grappling with significant reading barriers, school can become associated with repeated failure and isolation. The potential damage wrought by dyslexia is represented with painful honesty by Phillip Schultz, in his book, *My Dyslexia*:

> For a long time, I couldn't imagine my life amounting to anything ... I didn't know there was something wrong or different about how my brain processed information and language; I believed there was something wrong with me. I still, on occasion, believe this. Perhaps I always will.
>
> *My Dyslexia*, by Phillip Schultz, p. 117[11]

Phillip's story shares a raw truth regarding the enduring impact of severe reading barriers. In the face of a potentially crippling inability to access the school curriculum, along with the emotional and motivational damage this can elicit, there is understandably a desire to lessen the stigma around struggling readers.

Notions of dyslexia have often been associated with creativity in the face of such difficulties. An array of renowned geniuses that litter our history are cited as dyslexia success stories. From Pablo Picasso to Auguste Rodin, Agatha Christie to Walt Disney and from Steven Spielberg to Whoopi Goldberg, many famous people are deemed to be dyslexic. It has led to commonly held notions that dyslexia could actually prove a 'gift' and lead to success in innovative and unexpected ways.[12] The notion that the 'deliberate difficulty' of dyslexia could prove a boon offers a positive message for many of our struggling pupils.

Yet, we should be very wary of glamourising dyslexia. Alas, the 'gift of dyslexia' proves to be little more than an attractive fiction. In studies conducted at universities and elsewhere,[13] it was shown that there is no special creativity offered to dyslexic pupils to compensate for their other learning deficits. That isn't to say that dyslexic pupils cannot be tremendously creative and go on to flourish, but we should quash any notion that dyslexia could be desirable. We should address dyslexia as early and as comprehensively as we can.

So, what actually is dyslexia and how do we separate the fact from fiction?

We have known for well over a century that dyslexia has genetic roots.[14] Though it often runs in families[15] (a useful risk factor to try and identify in liaison with the families of our pupils) dyslexia is a heterogenous condition. That is to say, it can be influenced by various genetic and environmental factors.

Put simply, reading is a complex skill to develop and learn, so dyslexia proves a complex reading disorder.

The dominant scientific consensus view of dyslexia is that it is the result of a phonological deficit whereat the dyslexic brain struggles to match sounds to letters with accuracy.[16] During the act of reading, persistent small delays in processing sounds and words aggregates with damaging consequences. A few milliseconds late recognising a word, wedded to a few milliseconds attempting to connect that word to their store of background knowledge, all adds up to a slow, effortful and often fractured reading experience.

The report by Sir Jim Rose to government in 2009, *Identifying and Teaching Children and Young People with Dyslexia and Literacy Difficulties,* helpfully offered what is a widely known definition of dyslexia:

> Dyslexia is a learning difficulty that primarily affects the skills involved in accurate and fluent word reading and spelling.

- Characteristic features of dyslexia are difficulties in phonological awareness, verbal memory and verbal processing speed.
- Dyslexia occurs across the range of intellectual abilities.
- It is best thought of as a continuum, not a distinct category, and there are no clear cut-off points.
- Co-occurring difficulties may be seen in aspects of language, motor co-ordination, mental calculation, concentration and personal organisation, but these are not, by themselves, markers of dyslexia.

> *Identifying and Teaching Children and Young People with Dyslexia and Literacy Difficulties,*
> by Sir Jim Rose, pp. 9–10[17]

Unfortunately, there remains a great deal of contention about dyslexia that isn't very helpful for teachers looking for clear guidance. Phonological awareness itself exists on a continuum, so the issue of dyslexia is not clear-cut. One major debate regards how common dyslexia actually proves in our classrooms. Estimates can range from as high as 20%;[18] however the majority of experts place the figure for those pupils suffering from dyslexia at nearer 8% to 4%.[19]

The reading expert Mark Seidenberg, in his book *Language at the Speed of Sight: How We Read, Why So Many Can't, and What Can Be Done About It,* offers a helpful medical analogy. He states that when a person is diagnosed with mumps it proves a disease with a specific cause and little ambiguity, but that "dyslexia is not like the mumps".[20] Instead, he argues it is like hypertension or obesity. They are both recognised conditions by medical professionals, but they rest on a continuum and the exact causes can be complex, with multiple co-occurring issues. This then confounds any easy judgement or solution for teachers. We need to work that little bit harder to diagnose what supports our pupils require.

When commonly held myths about dyslexia clash with unclear boundaries and rather muddy categorisation, what are teachers to think? Whether we should use the term dyslexia at all has been disputed.[21] Aiming to discern dyslexia issues takes confidence and knowledge. We should first focus on encouraging intelligent diagnostic assessments in class, rather than jumping to diagnosing pupils with a broad label and assuming extra time in exams and coloured paper[22] will fill in the cracks in their reading competency. They won't. When an easy solution is proposed for a complex problem, like coloured paper for dyslexic readers, we should assume it is too good to be true.

Unless we address the gap in teacher knowledge regarding teaching reading, and reading barriers, we are unlikely to satisfactorily address our pupils' reading gaps.

For example, teachers with knowledge about the complexity of academic texts and pupils' reading barriers, can undertake diagnostic assessments like checking a pupil can accurately read words from an opening paragraph of a new text, by explicitly questioning about words and spelling patterns, or deploying a 'ready reckoner' with knowledge of the class in mind. Better this than teachers floundering and trying to use an expensive rainbow of coloured paper because a pupil is labelled dyslexic, without actually mediating the challenge of reading or focusing on teaching pupils to read more accurately and fluently.

Seidenberg aptly describes dyslexia as a "moving target".[23] And yet, the more we know and understand about how children learn to read, how they read to learn, and what accounts for text complexity, we can better fire at that self-same target and support our pupils.

We know that children who arrive at school with poor oral language skills are at risk of reading difficulties.[24] We know a family history is an obvious risk factor for our pupils. Early indicators can include a difficulty in repeating novel words (such as the non-words in the phonics check – 'skap' and 'blorn' from Chapter 3). Also, issues relate to poor phonological awareness – for example, differentiating the omitted phoneme between 'track' and 'tack' – can be subtle but important indicators.

Early identification of reading barriers can seek out dyslexia and much more. We know that narrow aspects of language knowledge matter greatly to reading development. For example, letter knowledge upon joining school is an effective predictor of reading success at the end of year 1.[25] Also, year 1 pupils who couldn't spell the following apparently simple words – 'hut', 'star', 'fork', 'ball', 'vest', 'crown' and 'star' – were deemed 'at risk' pupils.[26]

For older pupils, a vocabulary deficit can arise from weak early reading skill. This is then compounded further by avoiding reading activities for pleasure and leisure.[27] Pupils may be able to express themselves verbally, but simply cannot record the self-same ideas in their writing.[28] Of course, if you have suffered through reading with difficulty for year after year, your motivation as an adolescent reader can be simply rock bottom, sapping the pleasure from every corner of the school day. With poor motivation comes stunted practice and a vicious downward cycle ensues, so assessing motivation can be helpful and illuminating.[29]

Just for a moment, consider the pupils, like Phillip Schultz, who have dragged themselves through school feeling an abject failure. How well did they mask those feelings? How many times did they volunteer to read in class? How many times did they act like they were reading during 'silent reading' and similar?

It would be alluring to think that if we simply used coloured paper and coloured overlays we would address the issue of reading barriers for our dyslexic pupils. Alas, the evidence for the efficacy of dyslexic pupils using coloured paper is very weak.[30] Instead, we need to better support our pupils with high-quality, explicit teaching of reading based on deep professional knowledge.

The best indicators show that approaches related to teaching structured phonics, alongside teachers supporting pupils with reading-age-appropriate texts and reinforcing reading strategies, can best support dyslexic readers. In primary school (particularly in the earlier years), both these processes would be part of regular classroom instruction. In secondary school, it is much more likely that the reading support can happen with the teacher (especially in secondary English, but certainly not exclusively), but that structured phonics interventions would occur outside of the classroom. Across both phases of schooling, using 'fix-up strategies' and emphasising comprehension monitoring is likely to also aid dyslexic readers.

We return to the reading science of Chapter 3 and the focus on comprehension in Chapter 4. Pupils who are dyslexic, or simply struggling below their peers, benefit from explicit, structured instruction. Whether it is developing reading fluency, or the explicit teaching of reading strategies and vocabulary, a well-structured approach to developing reading benefits every pupil, harms no one, and those who struggle with reading gain the most.

The hidden problem of poor comprehenders

The reading condition termed dyslexia is well known and prompts interest, advocacy and interventions in equal measure. But what if there was another reading deficit experienced by a significant proportion of pupils that we have heard very little of before?

For many pupils, the reading barrier associated with dyslexia – the inability to read words accurately and fluently – is an inadequate explanation for their struggles reading in the classroom.[31] They can accurately read the words on the page, but they struggle to understand much of what is being read. Researchers pose that as many as 8% of such pupils in our classes could be described as 'poor comprehenders'.[32]

The diagnosis of 'poor comprehenders' is more like dyslexia than mumps: it is complex, with a range of complex causes and an unclear cut off to differentiate between pupils. For teachers, it can be particularly hard to spot poor comprehenders, given they can decode fluently and may sound very much like they are good readers. It can take time and carefully selected comprehension questions to draw back the veil on their gaps in understanding.

Is this issue a gap in your professional knowledge?

We can detect for many pupils the issue of poor reading comprehension as it reveals itself in oral language issues as early as upon school entry. For some children, they can struggle with listening comprehension. That is to say, understanding the meaning of words and the syntax of sentences; narrative skills – such as expressing yourself coherently, explaining actions or the flow of stories; and have limited vocabulary knowledge.

Without lots of rich oral language input before school, pupils simply don't have the foundations for accessing and making comprehensible what they read. Happily, there are strong interventions schools can access for such children in the Early Years, such as the 'Nuffield Early Language Programme'.[33]

As described in the previous chapter on reading comprehension, successful readers are knowledgeable, practised, highly active and strategic. Conversely, poor comprehenders don't use the aforementioned 'reduce/repair strategies' as effectively, such as rereading, questioning and noticing text structures:

> They do not see reading as an active, constructive process: It is only when their incorrect answer and therefore inadequate understanding is brought to their attention and they are required to search for some information, that these children make such links.
>
> 'Comprehension Skills and Inference-Making Ability: Issues of Causality', by K. Cain and J. V. Oakhill, p. 339[34]

The role of the teacher becomes paramount for such pupils. The explicit teaching of reading in every key stage and subject domain proves essential, not some bolt-on addition titled as 'literacy across the curriculum' or similar.

Though its roots can be founded in oral language from before school even starts, reading-comprehension difficulty tends to become more visible around 8 years of age,[35] as the complexity of what is being read increases. In the United States, there is a parallel thread of research that describes the 'fourth-grade slump'.[36] This describes the struggle of 10- and 11-year-olds as they read more complex texts. The reasoning is complex – likely resulting from a mix of factors.[37] There is the challenge of new, more complex vocabulary, while pupils are still trying to grapple with reading words fluently, alongside the reading in school demanding a good deal more background knowledge, with new, more complex sentence and whole-text structures.

Whereas the teaching of phonics is largely constrained to high-quality teaching in the classroom, your knowledge of the world can be strongly influenced by your family and social background.

Remember those empty bookshelves?

We can pre-empt comprehension failure, modelling and supporting our pupils' comprehension monitoring skill, while pre-teaching vocabulary and background knowledge we anticipate they may be lacking. First, the priority is to talk and ask questions to tease out their gaps in knowledge or their common misconceptions.

Through teaching strategies like targeted questioning and talk, we help our pupils monitor their reading comprehension. Asking questions that model inference making is crucial. Subtle, deep teacher knowledge of their pupils, and of reading development, matters here. Poor comprehenders find it harder to remember abstract words compared to concrete words,[38] so identification of such words by the teacher can help too. Teachers helping to connect those words up to visual hooks (think the abstraction of peace being inextricably linked to the image of the dove) can aid understanding and remembering.[39]

Some poor comprehenders may offer lots of classroom input when they read about a topic they know really well, but then hide beneath the radar during discussions about something that has been read when they are more reliant on understanding what they have specifically read.

Strategies that support pupils' memory are particularly helpful as poor comprehenders can have gaps in their background knowledge, coupled with a passive approach to reading, so the act of reading overwhelms their working memory (their ability to process new information as they read). And so, when poor comprehenders are faced with a complex passage of text they are less likely to remember and be able to repeat sentences than their peers.[40]

Actively foregrounding strategies to construct the jigsaw and remember the big picture of the text then becomes crucial for poor comprehenders.

Approaches like structured note-taking and using graphic organisers to represent the whole text – such as Venn diagrams, concept maps and fishbone diagrams – can help by consolidating and reconstructing the meaning of the text. Effectively, it is mental model building in visible terms. When a pupil reads a lot of text, or reads multiple sources, organising their thinking visually aids remembering and takes the load off the working memory of our novice pupils. For example, in year 5 geography, if pupils are researching their own city or town, they could devise a fishbone diagram to record some of the salient geographical categories, such as 'rural', 'urban', alongside 'housing' and 'land use', etc. (see Figure 5.1).

Akin to most issues with supporting pupils to overcome reading barriers, early support matters. There is a strong connection between early oral language and later reading comprehension. Research studies have shown that for young children, focusing on listening comprehension, vocabulary and narrative skills – responding with a trained adult to articulate and extend upon their ideas – provides the platform for later reading success.[41] For example, short, daily one-to-one interventions with teaching assistants[42] reveal the intricate relationship between talk and reading comprehension.

Researchers have helpfully begun to more specifically develop a 'poor comprehender profile'[43] that is useful for

Reading barriers

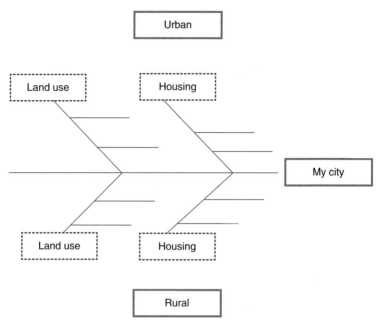

Figure 5.1   My city – fishbone diagram

teachers of every key stage and subject. The possible areas of difficulty they suggest are shown in the following table.

The 'simple view' for a complex problem

It is clear that if we are to ensure pupils like Matthew are to succeed, and gain the pleasure in reading that should be an intrinsic right for us all, then we need to know how language works and how reading can go wrong. It is a complex matter that will need teacher training, careful support and intelligent diagnostic assessments to close the gap.

A common model for diagnosing pupils' reading barriers is the ironically titled 'simple view of reading'.[44] It helpfully differentiates between the two major dimensions of

Potential reading barrier	Potential indicators in the classroom
Vocabulary	Uses limited vocabulary in speech and/or writing
Oral expression	Difficulty in organising verbal expression and/or limited engagement in class talk
Figurative language	Difficulty in fully appreciating layers of meaning, metaphor, jokes and wordplay
Narrative skills	Difficulty expressing experiences with narrative clarity or following sequences
Grammatical development	Difficulty following complex sentences, e.g. identifying the subject of the sentence, etc.
Verbal reasoning	Difficulty reasoning, e.g. identifying words that have similar or opposite meanings
Inferencing	Difficulty making inferences to cohere and elaborate upon what has been read
Comprehension monitoring	Difficulty recognising miscomprehensions or gaps in their knowledge
Verbal working memory	Difficulty following multi-step instructions
Motivation to read	Dislikes reading or selects from a very narrow range of books

Source: Adapted from *Developing Reading Comprehension*, by P. J. Clarke et al.

Reading barriers

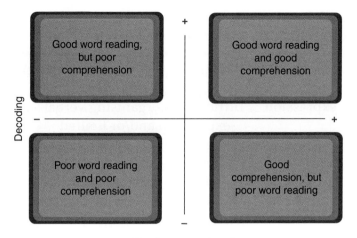

Figure 5.2 'Simple view of reading' quadrant

Source: Education Endowment Foundation (2017) *Improving Literacy in Key Stage 1*, London: Education Endowment Foundation.

reading: word reading, the ability to decode words correctly and nearly effortlessly and reading comprehension (see Figure 5.2).

A teacher identifying a weak reader just isn't helpful enough. We need to be much more specific about the learning barrier, but this takes knowledge of our pupils, of reading and of what specifically is being read. Is it an issue of word reading/decoding, or reading fluency? Is it an issue of reading fluency or reading comprehension?

These issues interact and can co-occur (such judgements will be limited and pupils don't easily fit neatly into scientific models and quadrants), of course, but by better understanding the issues, we can often zero in on more specific solutions and classroom practices.

Simply knowing that 'good word reading, but poor comprehension' could match a 'poor comprehender' profile, whereas 'good comprehension, but poor word reading' could relate to a dyslexia profile is a good start. It may lead to making better interventions, but also, crucially for teachers, useful decisions about what barriers pupils' face, which then provokes us to think about how we need to teach.

We can use the graphical version of the simple view to make small useful shortcuts about pupils in our class. Most pupils will invariably have good decoding and comprehension skills, but a proportion of pupils in KS2 and KS3 will have poor comprehension skills, with another group of pupils having weaker word-reading skills. We can ask where pupils in each class sit on the quadrant, knowing that such judgements will be flawed and limited, but ultimately useful.

Pupils like Matthew would invariably struggle in the bottom left-hand quadrant of the graph. Typically, this would require interventions above and beyond what the classroom teaching can offer. The well-established 'response to intervention'[45] model can further guide us to make judgements about the degrees of support pupils will need. They offer a three-wave model (see Figure 5.3).

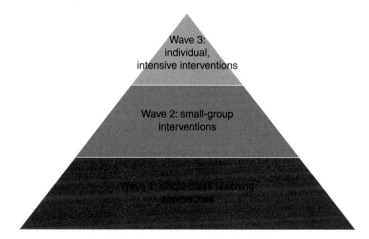

Figure 5.3　Waves of intervention

Reading barriers

If I was to have my time again reading with Matthew, I would implement a more structured approach to support his complex needs. I would seek to isolate and chunk down his barriers to reading, potentially going back to basics with decoding to secure his use of high-frequency vocabulary. I'd likely then work with him intensively on oral expression and reading fluency. It would require wave 1 intensity and focus.

It would likely be the case that working closely with a teaching assistant (TA) would require a partnership to support Matthew and the wider group.[46] The ideal scenario is that every teacher and TA would be highly trained, with the time to support one another, but too often this isn't the case. Given reading is so integral to accessing the school curriculum, it is imperative we find times in the school week to make reading access a primary concern.

For many of my successful teenage readers, I would still maintain a concerted focus on enhancing their comprehension, carefully sequencing what is being taught, for example developing their understanding of metaphorical language in English Literature. Alongside this, my text selection would explicitly take into account its relative difficulty for my pupils – being mindful to monitor the 'arduous eight' – rather than being bound to potentially limiting complexity formulas.

Whether it is by demystifying dyslexia, or by deconstructing what makes a text difficult, we can benefit every one of our pupils and help them to better access the school curriculum and close the reading gap.

IN SHORT ...

- Teachers can better support their pupils to over-come reading barriers by understanding what factors determine text complexity. Rather than rely on the limited tool of readability formulas, teachers can better understand the 'arduous eight' factors that characterise the sophisticated texts being read in school.

- Myths that glamourise dyslexia as a gift are dam-aging and false. We should concentrate our efforts on better understanding how to identify and address issues, such as word-reading difficulties, that best characterise the condition.

- Dyslexia is a moving target with no singular cause. As such, 'easy' solutions posed, like coloured paper, are unlikely to prove anywhere near suffi-cient to support pupils. We need instead to ensure our teaching of reading explicitly and effectively addresses specific issues, such as word reading and utilising 'reduce/repair strategies'.

- A less well-known issue than dyslexia is that of the issues experienced by 'poor comprehenders'. Experienced by as many as 8% of pupils, this con-dition is characterised by struggles with active monitoring of their comprehension and a failure to deploy apt 'reduce/repair strategies'.

- The 'simple view of reading' is a useful model to differentiate between different reading barriers, such as dyslexic pupils who struggle with decoding and those pupils who are poor comprehenders.

Notes

1 BBC News (2019). *Mr Greedy* 'almost as hard to read' as Steinbeck Classics. Retrieved from www.bbc.co.uk/news/uk-47426551.
2 Mullis, I. V. S., Martin, M. O., Foy, P., & Hooper, M. (2017). *PIRLS 2016 international results in reading.* Retrieved from http://timssandpirls.bc.edu/pirls2016/international-results.
3 Best, R. M., Floyd, R. G., & McNamara, D. (2008). Differential competencies contributing to children's comprehension of narrative and expository texts. *Reading Psychology, 29*(2), 137–164. https://doi.org/10.1080/02702710801963951.
4 Cain, K., Oakhill, J. V., & Elbro, C. (2003). The ability to learn new word meanings from context by school-age children with and without language comprehension difficulties. *Journal of Child Language, 30,* 681–694.
5 Cain, K., & Oakhill, J. V. (2007). Reading comprehension difficulties: Correlates, causes and consequences. In K. Cain & J. V. Oakhill (Eds.), *Children's comprehension problems in oral and written language* (pp. 41–75). New York, NY: Guilford Press.
6 AQA (2016), Our exams explained: GCSE science exams from Summer 2018. Retrieved from https://filestore.aqa.org.uk/resources/science/AQA-GCSE-SCIENCE-EXAMS-EXPLAINED.PDF.
7 AQA (2016). Making questions clear: GCSE Science exams from 2018. Retrieved from https://filestore.aqa.org.uk/resources/science/AQA-GCSE-SCIENCE-QUESTIONS-CLEAR.PDF, p. 6.
8 Ibid.
9 Tennant, W. (2014). *Understanding reading comprehension.* London: Sage.
10 Kispal, A. (2008). *Effective teaching of inference skills for reading: Literature review.* Department for Education Research Report. Retrieved from www.nfer.ac.uk/publications/EDR01/EDR01.pdf.
11 Schultz, P. (2011). *My dyslexia.* New York, NY: W. W. Norton & Company, p. 117.
12 Gladwell, M. (2014). *David and Goliath: Underdogs, misfits and the art of battling giants.* London: Penguin.

13 Łockiewicz, M., Bogdanowicz, K., & Bogdanowicz, M. (2013). Psychological resources of adults with developmental dyslexia. *Journal of learning disabilities, 47*(6), 543–555. doi:10.1177/0022219413478663.

14 Morgan, W. P. (1896). A case of congenital word blindness. *British Medical Journal, 2*(1871), 1378. doi:10.1136/bmj.2.1871.1378.

15 Paracchini, S., Scerri, T., & Monaco, A. P. (2007). The genetic lexicon of dyslexia. *Annual Review of Genomics Human Genetics, 8*, 57–79.

16 Vellutino, F. R., Fletcher, J. M., Snowling, M. J., & Scanlon, D. M. (2004). Specific reading disability (dyslexia): What have we learned from the past four decades? *Journal of Child Psychology Psychiatry, 45*(1), 2–40.

17 Rose, J. (2009). *Identifying and teaching children and young people with dyslexia and literacy difficulties.* An independent report from Sir Jim Rose to the Secretary of State for Children, Schools and Families. Retrieved from http://webarchive.nationalarchives.gov.uk/20130401151715/www.education.gov.uk/publications/eorderingdownload/00659-2009dom-en.pdf.

18 Shaywitz, S. E. (1996). Dyslexia. *Scientific American,* November, 98–104.

19 Snowling, M. J. (2008). Specific disorders and broader phenotypes: The case of dyslexia. *Quarterly Journal of Experimental Psychology, 61*(1), 142–156. https://doi.org/10.1080/17470210701508830.

20 Seidenberg, M. (2017). *Reading at the speed of sight: How we read, why so many can't, and what can be done about it.* New York, NY: Basic Books, p. 158.

21 Elliott, J. G., & Grigorenko, E. L. (2014). *The dyslexia debate.* New York, NY: Cambridge University Press.

22 Henderson, L. M., Tsogka, N., & Snowling, M. J. (2013). Questioning the benefits that coloured overlays can have for reading in students with and without dyslexia. *Jorsen, 13*, 57–65.

23 Seidenberg, M. (2017). *Reading at the speed of sight: How we read, why so many can't, and what can be done about it.* New York, NY: Basic Books.

24 Snowling, M. (2014). Dyslexia: A language learning impairment. *Journal of the British Academy, 2*, 43–58.

25 Walsh, D. J., Price, G. G., & Gillingham, M. G. (1988). The critical but transitory importance of letter naming. *Reading Research Quarterly, 23,*108–122.

26 Hatcher, P. J., Hulme, C., Miles, J. N. V., Carroll, J. M., Hatcher, J., Smith, G., & Gibbs, S. (2006). Efficacy of small-group reading intervention for beginning readers with reading delay: A randomised controlled trial. *Journal of Child Psychology & Psychiatry, 47*(8), 820–827. https://doi.org/10.1111/j.1469-7610.2005.01559.x.

27 Griffiths, Y. M., & Snowling, M. J. (2002). Predictors of exception word and nonword reading in dyslexic children: The severity hypothesis. *Journal of Educational Psychology, 94*(1), 34–43. http://dx.doi.org/10.1037/0022-0663.94.1.34.

28 Ibid.

29 Melekoglu, M. A., & Wilkerson, K. L. (2013). Motivation to read: How does it change for struggling readers with and without disabilities? *International Journal of Instruction, 6*(1), 77–88.

30 Suttle, C. M., Lawrenson, J. G., & Conway, M. L. (2018). Efficacy of coloured overlays and lenses for treating reading difficulty: An overview of systematic reviews. *Clinical and Experimental Optometry, 101*(4), 514–520.

31 Nation, K., Clarke, P., & Snowling, M. J. (2002). General cognitive ability in children with reading comprehension difficulties. *British Journal of Educational Psychology, 72*(4), 549–560. http://dx.doi.org/10.1348/00070990260377604; Cain, K., & Oakhill, J. V. (2006). Profiles of children with specific reading comprehension difficulties. *British Journal of Educational Psychology, 76*(4), 683–696. https://doi.org/10.1348/000709905X67610.

32 Clarke, P. J., Snowling, M. J., Truelove, E., & Hulme, C. (2010). Ameliorating children's reading comprehension difficulties: A randomised controlled trial. *Psychological Science, 21,* 1106–1116. doi:10.1177/0956797610375449.

33 Snowling, M. J. (2018). Language: The elephant in the reading room. Retrieved from https://readoxford.org/language-the-elephant-in-the-reading-room.

34 Cain, K., & Oakhill, J. V. (1998). Comprehension skills and inference-making ability: Issues of causality. In C. Hulme &

R. M. Joshi (Eds.), *Reading and spelling: Development and disorders* (pp. 329–242). Mahwah, NJ: Lawrence Erlbaum Associates.

35 Clarke, P. J., Truelove, E., Hulme, C., & Snowling, M. (2013). *Developing reading comprehension*. Chichester, UK: John Wiley & Sons.

36 Chall, J. S., Jacobs, V. A., & Baldwin, L. E. (1990). *The reading crisis: Why poor children fall behind*. Cambridge, MA: Harvard University Press.

37 Goodwin, B. (2011). Research says ... don't wait until 4th grade to address the slump. *Educational Leadership, 68*(7). Retrieved from www.ascd.org/publications/educational-leadership/apr11/vol68/num07/Don%27t-Wait-Until-4th-Grade-to-Address-the-Slump.aspx.

38 Marshall, C. M., & Nation, K. (2003). Individual differences in semantic and structural errors in children's memory for sentences. *Educational and Child Psychology, 20*(3), 7–18.

39 Gladfelter, I., Barron, K. L., & Johnson, E. (2019). Visual and verbal semantic productions in children with ASD, DLD, and typical language. *Journal of Communication Disorders, 82*(105921). https://doi.org/10.1016/j.jcomdis.2019.105921.

40 Ibid.

41 Fricke, S., Bowyer-Crane, C., Haley, A. J., Hulme, C., & Snowling, M. J. (2013). Efficacy of language intervention in the early years. *Journal of Child Psychology and Psychiatry, 54*(3), 280–290.

42 See it in action here: https://bit.ly/2GZWnGO.

43 Clarke, P. J., Truelove, E., Hulme, C., & Snowling, M. (2013). *Developing reading comprehension*. Chichester, UK: John Wiley & Sons, p. 25.

44 Gough, P. B., & Tunmer, W. E. (1986). Decoding, reading, and reading disability. *Remedial and Special Education, 7*, 6–10.

45 Burns, M. K., Appleton, J. J., & Stehouwer, J. D. (2005). Meta-analytic review of responsiveness-to-intervention research: Examining field-based and research-implemented models. *Journal of Psychoeducational Assessment, 23*, 381–394.

46 Education Endowment Foundation (2018). *Making best use of teaching assistants*. London: Education Endowment Foundation.

Reading in the subject disciplines

Take a moment to read the following two passages about lighthouses and consider their differences, similarities and where and when a pupil may encounter them in the school curriculum:

> For the great plateful of blue water was before her; the hoary lighthouse, distant, austere in the midst; and on the right, as far as the eye could see, fading and falling, in soft low pleats, the green sand dunes with the wild flowing grasses on them.
>
> *To the Lighthouse*, by Virginia Woolf, p. 13[1]

> Belle Toute lighthouse is a famous landmark on the top of the cliffs at Beachy Head, on the South coast of England … erosion of the cliff has continued since the lighthouse was moved back, and a series of wet winters and very dry summers has caused the erosion to speed up.
>
> 'Coasts Lesson Plans: Look at It This Way Lesson 8', by the Geographical Association[2]

As an expert reader, with countless years of expertise reading in a range of genres and subject disciplines, you will have very likely found this a relatively easy and seemingly 'natural' task. All that knowledge that isn't explicitly set out on the page you bring to the text. The many inferences you can make from the word choices, the syntax and the style are near instantaneously brought to bear to enlighten our comprehension of these two short texts.

You will likely have noted the key similarity: that both texts share the subject of a lighthouse. Probably, you then focused upon the salient differences: the genre of the first text appears to be literary fiction; whereas the second text appears to be an informational text. The word choices help us make these global inferences. Poetic sounding phrases like "wild flowing grasses" can be contrasted with the functional but informative "erosion of the cliff".

Though we may not be self-professed grammar experts, we note that the first text utilises a plethora of adjectives and verbs and a sentence structure with lots of seemingly fluid, interconnected clauses. It is a literary text – but you likely already knew that – from the novel by Virginia Woolf, *To the Lighthouse*. It is sophisticated, with mature themes and the attendant vocabulary, such as "austere", hinting that older pupils would read such a text.

When viewing this text through the lens of a literary critic and fiction reader, we instinctively begin a new way of reading in role. We seek out symbolism. We make inferences that the sentence structure may be imitating the flow of water upon the lighthouse and much more. As reading experts, we draw upon a literary tradition that includes symbolism, from Odysseus' journey home to the green light at the end of Jay Gatsby's dock.

In contrast, the second text is part of a KS3 lesson plan from the Geographical Association on the theme of coasts. It is one of a range of texts, including images of the coast, a lighthouse, an estate agent's advertisement, as well as a collection of quotes from local people. These informational texts can be compared and corroborated to evoke a distinctive sense of place. 'Place making' becomes the reading comprehension strategy utilised by geographers to characterise the making of their mental model. The emphasis on "erosion" infers that pupils will need to quickly embed in their mental model this important concept in physical geography, such as the four different types of erosion and related coastal processes.

By paying attention to the specialised ways of reading, knowing and doing, in each subject discipline,[3] we can recognise that there are both general reading skills and subject-specialist strategies that our pupils need to develop. This approach is termed 'disciplinary literacy'. It differs from more common approaches to 'literacy across the curriculum',[4] in that it emphasises there are useful general literacy skills and reading strategies, but that this is almost always mediated within a subject discipline, so we need to attend to those nuanced differences.

Clearly, how we read differs depending upon the text, the purpose for reading and the subject domain. We read differently as a geographer than we do as a literary critic; we can read the same text differently again as a biologist or as an artist. We have different aims, roles and goals every time we read. We do so by typically drawing from well-established subject domains and their ways of reading, seeing and thinking. Developing this specialist knowledge as we read begins early and develops as pupils mature across primary and secondary school.

As soon as a pupil has mastered learning to read, reading to learn initiates this lengthy but vital process of discerning the specialness of reading in the subject disciplines. With careful attention to 'disciplinary literacy', we can best support our pupils to flourish as readers in the classroom as they progress through each key stage.

Reading with a subject lens and spying informational text trends

How does a geographer read?

This is a vital question for geography teachers. Yet, it would be surprising if this topic was allocated space in whole-school training in primary or secondary schools, given it is highly specialised knowledge and the assumption is that such knowledge is just acquired and develops in our classrooms. Given the sheer breadth of the primary school curriculum, such nuanced, seemingly marginal questions simply aren't likely to be asked either. And so, potential curriculum connectedness across key phases and schools regarding academic reading is usually a prize that goes unclaimed.

But what if attending to the ways of reading and knowing in this way proved integral to school success? With an attention on 'disciplinary literacy' in primary and secondary schools, could we establish a platform for such marginal questions to shape reading, our classroom practice and curriculum design?

We can define the complex act of reading like a geographer. First, given the task of reading a case study or information about a geographical phenomenon, such as erosion, a geographer would apply an analytical perspective that can encompass a range of viewpoints, e.g.

- political perspectives;
- environmental perspectives;
- social perspectives;
- economic perspectives.

By framing reading through these lenses, we can offer our novice pupils an apt scaffold to collate ideas, make annotations and plan in response to their reading. Akin to 'reciprocal reading', in Chapter 4, we can allocate roles and goals to focus pupils' reading. Such a strategy can start as early as primary school, with writing scaffolds and classroom display materials orientated to aid reading through the lens of a geographer in this way.

A geographer seeks out trends and patterns with these viewpoints in mind. These reading goals are met by seeking out a more specialised collection of texts. A geographer who is posed a question about sub-Saharan Africa may need to draw upon the reading of maps, statistics and personal accounts, to better establish the interrelationship between the respective human systems and the physical environment. As explored in the previous chapter, a primary school pupil tasked with investigating their local area will likely access a range of text genres that they need to read concurrently and cross-reference, such as websites, informational books and advertisements, etc. As such, reading in geography is uniquely challenging but also rewarding in its uniqueness.

Knowledge of place, from river basins to glacial ice, is crucial, but this is more than listing a series of capital cities. Foregrounding specialist geographical language helps pupils accurately understand geographical texts. 'Mouth', 'delta', 'tributary', 'confluence' and 'source', all invoke a clear sense of place for a geographer. These words connect visual map reading with their linguistic equivalents. Reading multimodal texts (that is to say, a text with more than one mode, e.g. a website with words, images and hyperlinks) then proves integral to reading like a geographer.

Ideally, primary school teachers and their secondary school colleagues would work in unison to develop the parameters of 'reading like a geographer', 'reading like a biologist' and more, within a coherent curriculum development model. By combining our expertise of sub-ject knowledge[5] and our knowledge of reading[6] (primary teachers can often be more expert in reading than their secondary subject specialist peers), we can find valuable solutions to reading in every classroom.

A curriculum map can include an ordered sequence of big ideas, concepts and subject-specific vocabulary. We can map the micro detail of important vocabulary, along-side the macro decisions that attend extended reading text choices. We can also identify 'essential' and 'additional' reading for topics, ensuring we map our desirable wider reading that would add richness to our pupils' required background knowledge.

Though there is much to be gained from asking questions that tease out the uniqueness of subject-specific reading, we can identify common features of reading informational texts that would be useful for every teacher to know and inform the overarching map of the school curriculum.

Informational texts – so dominant in our pupils' reading experience in secondary school in particular, but also vitally important as pupils move through primary school – share common structures. To be a successful and strategic reader, our pupils need to be knowledgeable about these different text structures[7] (especially given informational texts are typically more difficult for our pupils when compared to comprehending narrative texts[8]). There are five structures that are common for informational texts:[9]

1. **Description**: A text where the author simply describes something, e.g. a description of an animal habitat in biology.
2. **Sequence**: A text where the description is explicitly ordered sequentially, e.g. a chronological timeline in history.

3. **Cause and effect**: A text where the author describes relationships between events and their outcomes, e.g. a physics text that describes Newton's laws of motion.
4. **Compare and contrast**: A text where the author illuminates understanding by comparison and making connections, e.g. in an art text, two artistic periods may be compared.
5. **Problem and solution**: A text where the author illuminates connections between a problem and a solution, e.g. in food technology, the issue of unhealthy eating with solutions regarding making informed choices about a balanced diet.

A pupil being guided to identify overall text structures helps them with reasoning and understanding. When familiarity with these structures grows, pupils can more actively identify the most salient information, skimming and scanning, quickly cohering what they read. The key to understanding complex texts – often masked with technical vocabulary and a high density of facts – is to identify their underlying patterns and structures. Effectively, we are always helping our pupils navigate a complex map of meaning.

We can signpost our pupils to spy the discourse markers (remember the 'cohesive ties' from Chapter 1?) that consistently organise academic texts, as shown in the following table.

With timely and concise teacher modelling, identifying these patterns in texts can be done in an instant. For example, a geography text that describes a process like erosion would likely prove a combination of 'description', 'sequence' and 'cause and effect'. If we were to guide our pupils in annotating such a text, then they can better chunk down their reading into steps or identifying the

Description	Sequence	Cause and effect	Compare and contrast	Problem and solution
For example ...	First ...	Because ...	Similarly ...	Consequently ...
For instance ...	Second ...	Due to ...	Likewise ...	Therefore ...
Moreover ...	Third ...	If ... then ...	In the	As a result ...
Furthermore	Next ...	So ...	same way ...	To resolve this ...
... Also ...	Then ...	Therefore ...	Equally ...	If ... then ...
Additionally ...	Subsequently ...	Thus ...	Akin to ...	So that ...
Such as ...	Furthermore ...	Consequently ...	Alternatively ...	
Notably ...	Finally ...	Hence ...	Conversely ...	
	In conclusion ...		On the other	
			hand ...	
			In contrast ...	
			Instead ...	

key causes of erosion in the given text. Diagrams, flow charts and other visual methods of organisation map on to these different text structures. Teachers and pupils can then more easily pick the right tool for the job, e.g. flow charts for sequential texts; fishbone diagrams for cause and effect texts and so on.

It is important that pupils read extended texts if they are to grow more sensitive to text structures. If they are predominantly reading PowerPoint slides with condensed phrases, sentences and images, they will not gain experience in tracking more extended text structures. Paradoxically, by making the curriculum more accessible in the short term, we can make it harder to access curriculum reading in the long term. There is also some evidence that for struggling readers, reading extended fiction texts at a faster pace can prove more effective than aiming to slow reading down and inserting activities in an attempt to make it bite-size and accessible.[10]

At Allerton Grange School in Leeds, the head of history, Tim Jenner, has attempted to make 'reading routine'[11] in a systematic way, wedding more challenging wider reading to the rich historical enquiries being undertaken in class. By carefully planning a curriculum that first promoted more familiar narrative-focused texts by historians, while promoting 'core texts' for each enquiry, Jenner focused on a careful development of reading more extended extracts of historical scholarship. The aims were not nice extras for Jenner, but integral to learning:

> To help pupils handle a greater degree of complexity in the narratives they encountered. Longer texts do not neatly give up their answers to be easily digested and regurgitated by pupils. Instead, they require pupils to

grapple with complex narratives and deal with a degree of nuance rarely encountered in textbooks.

'Making Reading Routine: Helping KS3 Pupils
to Become Regular Readers of Historical
Scholarship', by Tim Jenner, p. 43[12]

By setting up 'lending libraries', promoting reading of articles, magazines, books and more, we help our pupils to reach beyond the bare limits of the prescribed curriculum. The background knowledge required for reading comprehension often resides in the hinterland[13] that is too often hidden from view when faced with a sequence of disembodied short extracts of text.

Put simply, you learn to 'read like a historian' by reading a lot of great historians widely and as deeply as possible.

Though the science curriculum at every key stage threatens to burst at the seams of the school timetable, it can be the wider reading of informational texts that builds the platform for comprehending the abstract science concepts that many pupils can struggle to comprehend. Sources like the Royal Society Young People's Book Prize offer a range of past winners and shortlisted books that can offer us a potent reading curriculum.[14]

Doug Lemov has termed 'pre-complex texts'[15] as those that helpfully introduce difficult concepts and topics before they are introduced to the more sophisticated reading equivalent in the classroom. This can work well in subjects as diverse as science, history and English literature.

We should then find, devise, curate and share such reading lists so that our pupils gain access to the breadth and depth of reading that is required to flourish in school and far beyond the school gates.

Tackling textbooks

> Let me control the textbooks and I will control the state.
>
> Attributed to Adolf Hitler[16]

In their various guises, textbooks have existed as long as organised education. No doubt, in the Sumerian classroom, bunches of tablets scratched in cuneiform will have been stored by the assiduous teacher to record the knowledge required of the young boys' learning.

Though technological advances threaten the primacy of the paper textbook – from the rise of PowerPoint, to the promise of interactive, electronic texts – it still forms an integral part of academic reading in school.

Textbooks have long since been bound to the more formal parameters of the national curriculum. Though governments have long since been attempting to influence and even to control textbooks (more recently, and not without controversy, the Department for Education has approved a single primary maths textbook[17]), our pupils (indeed teachers) can often prove passive and uncritical when faced with textbooks. We need to ensure that our pupils can confidently navigate the unique structures of textbooks (alongside worksheets, booklets and similar) and therefore act as active, strategic readers.

The explicit teaching of reading textbooks will likely make our pupils better readers and help them better access the challenging informational texts that are densely presented within the textbook. Consider how the following strategies can foster a more strategic approach to reading textbooks:

- **Considering chapter titles**: Read the contents list and consider what is the most significant chapter and why? This gets pupils actively classifying and ordering topics within the text. It can help pupils identify whether the text is ordered chronologically or conceptually. It also activates their prior knowledge signalled by the chapter titles.

- **Getting to grips with the glossary**: Faced with the textbook glossary, pose pupils the following questions: *What three words are most familiar? What three words are least unfamiliar?* This simple activity prompts pupils to calibrate their background knowledge[18] and primes their interest, while offering useful feedback for the teacher. It also, usefully, gets them actually *using* the glossary.
- **Confidence calibration**: Our pupils can be overconfident when faced with new topics.[19] A handy way to tease this out into the open – to be discussed and interrogated – is to get pupils to score themselves and their prior knowledge related to each topic/chapter in the textbook.
- **20 textbook questions**: Given a new chapter or topic posed by the textbook, get pupils to generate as many questions as possible. This helps to activate their prior knowledge, with the quality of the questions revealing what they know, what they are intrigued by and much more. They also provide a tool to return to that can be a great marker for progress.
- **Finding helpful text features**: Pupils are asked to scan the text and list the five most helpful text features that are utilised by the author/s. This strategy offers the opportunity for the teacher to reinforce the support structures, such as the glossary, which can simply go unused by weaker, less confident readers of all ages.

These classroom approaches can help ensure that the structures and organisational scaffolds that are common to textbooks do not remain implicit, thereby widening the gap between confident, strategic readers and their weaker peers. They make features explicit, such as how textbooks organise knowledge sequentially, while foregrounding important generic supports like the glossary, diagrams, embedded tasks and more.

In concrete terms, you can see the ever-present challenge faced by pupils when faced with a chemistry GCSE textbook (see Figure 6.1).

Clearly, pupils who advance through secondary school aiming to 'read like a scientist' must grapple with the unique feature of how scientific knowledge is represented in a way that younger readers do not. For example, carbon can be represented by the word in different ways:

$$\text{Carbon} = \text{C} = [\text{He}]\ 2s^2 2p^2$$

Not only that, pupils need to know that carbon is a non-metal element, that the human body is about 20% carbon, as well as its existence in different forms, such as graphite, diamond and graphene. The ample background knowledge that is not explicit in the text needs to be brought to bear by the pupil. Indeed, when faced with such examples, the academic language faced by older pupils can appear to be as densely packed as the carbon atoms in the crystal structure of a diamond.

By unlocking the dense, often tacit, text structures of textbooks for our pupils, we help them to be active, strategic readers. They can then begin to 'read to learn' and develop the wealth of knowledge required for school success.

Reading like …

What do Lucy Worsley, Professor David Olusoga and Professor Mary Beard have in common?

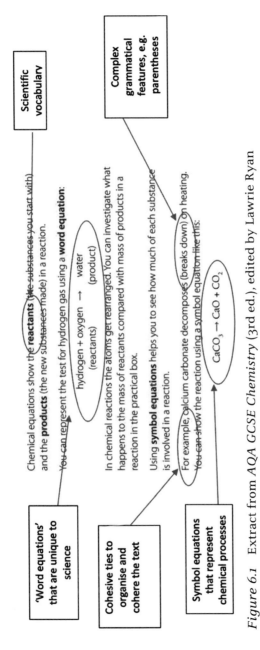

Scientific vocabulary

Complex grammatical features, e.g. parentheses

Chemical equations show the **reactants** (the substances you start with) and the **products** (the new substances made) in a reaction.

You can represent the test for hydrogen gas using a **word equation**:

hydrogen + oxygen → water
(reactants)   (product)

In chemical reactions the atoms get rearranged. You can investigate what happens to the mass of reactants compared with mass of products in a reaction in the practical box.

Using **symbol equations** helps you to see how much of each substance is involved in a reaction.

For example, calcium carbonate decomposes (breaks down) on heating. You can show the reaction using a symbol equation like this:

$$CaCO_3 \rightarrow CaO + CO_2$$

'Word equations' that are unique to science

Cohesive ties to organise and cohere the text

Symbol equations that represent chemical processes

Figure 6.1 Extract from *AQA GCSE Chemistry* (3rd ed.), edited by Lawrie Ryan

As well as being esteemed historians, they all share the task of carefully crafting narratives for television viewers of their history documentaries. When they pick up a history book – well, they'll take on the stance of a historian. They'll pursue patterns of change and causality over time, just like a primary school pupil comparing and contrasting the reigns of Queen Elizabeth I and Queen Elizabeth II.[20] The language they use will usually be more sophisticated than that of the pupils – revealing obvious novice and expert differences – but the lens of being a historian is a shared stance and a distinctive way of reading and thinking.

We can apply the specific reading lens to every subject domain. By combining general reading strategies, like comprehension monitoring and inference making, alongside subject-specific reading strategies, such as a historian sourcing and corroborating, we 'read like a historian'. Of course, *how* we read is combined with our background knowledge of *what* we read (see Figure 6.2).

Mathematics

Mathematics is seldom the subject discipline we associate with reading. Indeed, traditional notions of reading appear to clash with the real work of maths teachers, as it seldom relies on words, sentences and acts of extended reading[21] as have predominantly been described in this book. And yet, we know that the act of reading maths is difficult and important.

Reading the unique language of mathematics has even been described as tantamount to "reading Tolstoy's *Anna Karenina* in the original Russian".[22] Indeed, it is argued that maths texts have "more concepts per word, per sentence, per paragraph, than any other area."[23] Lots of reading from

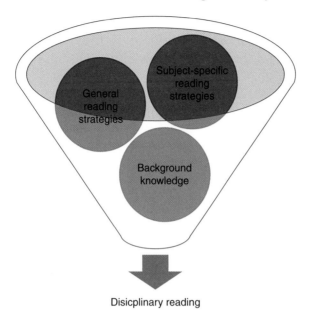

Disicplinary reading

Figure 6.2   Disciplinary reading

other curriculum areas won't necessarily help, given that over half of the vocabulary used in maths texts aren't used as frequently in other non-maths texts.[24]

A simple example of pupils struggling with maths word problems was shared with me by a primary headteacher colleague, Mari Palmer. She described how she had used a fractions problem shared by secondary colleagues with her primary school class. The question involved the fractions of a 'whole rod'. The problem? For three pupils in her class, they were left perplexed and looking everywhere for a diagram with a fishing rod!

Reading maths poses multiple problems and potential barriers for pupils. They can possess strong number bonds and algorithm skills, but then they concurrently have to decipher word problems, translate the words into operations and more. They can simply be overloaded when reading a word problem if they are not secure with their mathematical knowledge. The challenges are multifaceted:

- Pupils can find it difficult to move between text and graphics.[25]
- Pupils can find maths vocabulary difficult given some words have highly specific meanings only found in maths (e.g. isosceles), whereas other words have very wide common use but a different meaning in maths (e.g. prime, factor). Alongside this, some maths terms sound like familiar words, but are not (pi – not pie!).
- Pupils have to interpret words to find the appropriate mathematical symbol, so 'increase', 'positive', 'add' and 'more' can denote '+'.[26]
- Pupils can easily confuse related mathematical terms, e.g. denominator and numerator.[27]

Given the many subtle, near-hidden barriers when reading mathematics, it is important that we read with precision. Error detection, so vital to maths problems and proofs, can only really be addressed by our pupils possessing deep background knowledge of maths and proving strategic, meticulous readers. Rereading may well prove the key maths reading strategy. As pupils read and reread a question, they are trying to understand words, sifting for significant meaning and removing what is irrelevant to the problem.

We can guide them to reread with a 'scan, step and secure' triple read. The first step – 'scan' – sees pupils quickly survey the words and sentences in the problem to identify key words that may indicate operations (for example, 'decreased by' and 'fewer' would likely indicate subtraction). Then, for the second read, pupils look for 'steps' in the question. There are likely multiple steps, so making notes or using diagrams will aid this second read. Finally, they undertake a read to 'secure' understanding and read explicitly for error detection.

History

In an age of 'fake news', teaching pupils to 'read like a historian' may be one of the best antidotes we can administer. With the neutral, objective, enquiry-led, fact-checking stance of the historian, we pose an approach to reading that is required in our information-rich age, but that too often can prove rare.

For pupils in our classrooms, the reading stance and role of a historian are clear. They read a range of texts with the aim of developing 'period sensitivity'[28] – that is to say, a rich mental model of a period in the past – recognising patterns of change and continuity over time. Simplistic notions of history as a litany of disconnected facts and timelines – or 'memory history' – as described by Leverque, should be replaced by reading extended historical scholarship and sources with sensitivity to reconstructing, interrogating and interpreting rich historical narratives.

This stance takes attention to the act of reading. Historians deploy their own unique reading strategies:[29]

- **Sourcing**: Pupils deliberate over the author of the source and the conditions of its creation, asking questions like: Who wrote this and what message were they intending to convey – either implicitly or explicitly?
- **Contextualising**: Pupils root the source in the time and place, seeking to understand how social, political forces influenced the text etc., asking questions like: Who was the intended audience of the text?

- **Corroborating**: Pupils then corroborate the source with a range of related sources to gain the necessary 'period sensitivity', asking questions like: What is the relative reliability of the source in comparison to X?

Pupils who read as historians become sensitive to the language of historical claims. The voice of a historian is duly tentative, using modal verbs such as 'may', 'could' and 'might'. Specific concepts important to historians – such as change and continuity – are attended by a familiar field of language e.g. 'revive', 'remain', subvert', 'parallel' and 're-establish'.[30]

To gain the required sensitivity to source work in history begins early. It requires considerable practice reading historical scholarship to understand how to read like a historian, but equally, it takes explicit teaching of reading to make the implicit patterns and reading strategies explicit to our novice pupils.

English

The English classroom is largely considered the home of reading. In primary school, it is reading lessons when the act of strategic reading is foregrounded; in secondary school English, it is typically the study of English literature when teachers pay attention to what we deem 'close reading' (the careful, precise exploration of layers of meaning). Such practices can range from analysing short extracts to extended literary texts.

Even within the English community the notions of how we read and why we read are variable and contested. Over time, the reading of literature has developed a thriving array of children's literature, while academia has cycled through various critical theories and approaches that effectively approach a piece of literature with a particular stance.

Established critical perspectives have taken root in the classroom more than others, such as 'reader-response theory'. That is to say, it is the emotional and psychological response of the reader that is essential. Effectively: "Literature equals book plus reader".[31] When we write a poem in response to reading Blake's London, we are evoking such a critical perspective. Researchers have helpfully scrutinised how young readers approach fiction. Protherough[32] helpfully categorises the five ways children discover texts:

1. Projection into a character.
2. Projection into the situation.
3. Association between book and reader.
4. The distanced viewer.
5. The detached evaluation.

We can see these different stances/roles at work implicitly when undertaking tasks in response to fiction, such as 1, 2 and 3, when writing literature in response to what has been read, whereas 4 and 5 better align with an analytical essay response. Pupils can benefit from understanding these various critical roles and how we may engage with reading fiction in different ways.

What we can agree on about reading in English is that we are not hunting for logic, like in science and mathematics, but instead there is a search for ambiguity,[33] with singular interpretations being actively resisted when reading literature. This can be a shock for novice readers, who can be happy with singular meanings and do not think to elaborate any further.[34] Recurring patterns of metaphors, motifs and symbolism can prove tricky for those pupils who haven't read a broad wealth of literature, so reading quality, in quantity, really does matter.

We can also agree that we should foreground the deep structures and patterns – the full mental model – of great literature. Whether it is patterns woven by genre, such as the 'seven basic plots',[35] or Propp's character archetypes or literacy themes over time, we can help our pupils cohere the vast wealth of great literature. By connecting such intricate patterns together, what can emerge is the prototype design for our curriculum plans within and across both primary and secondary school.

Modern foreign languages (MFL)

The study of modern foreign languages (MFL) can be of immense value to our pupils, helping them connect themselves to the vast wealth of cultures and peoples of the world. Given that even pupils in secondary school will typically lack the breadth of vocabulary that allows for extended reading in a second language, it is understandable that reading isn't central. Instead, speaking and listening is prioritised in the classroom.

Arguably, "reading texts are often under-exploited"[36] in MFL. Though there is no doubt excellent practice in many MFL classrooms, a deep knowledge of how children learn to read can further support MFL teachers. To successfully learn a second language, adequate decoding is crucial.[37] Uniquely, decoding ability in English can paradoxically prove a barrier given the different patterns of sound in other languages. For example, the /o/ sound in English – as used in low (l/o/w) – has different letter/sound combinations in French, such as 'bat**eau**', '**f**au**x**', 'dr**ô**le'. It is important therefore that MFL addresses decoding – going back to the building blocks of reading.

Recent research in KS3 classes has indicated phonics teaching can aid vocabulary development in a second language (French).[38] The researchers also recommended combining phonics instruction with the teaching of reading strategies, while building motivation and challenge by using more challenging reading over "shorter, simpler and more predictable kinds of texts".[39]

Low motivation to read is an issue in MFL. Pupils are invariably faced with short, uninspiring reading texts, twinned with bland comprehension questions. Of course, structures to support such richer, more extended reading approaches like the 'reciprocal reading' structure, could make the aim more viable.

— — —

These subject-specific pen portraits can only touch the surface of the subjects outlined, while they don't represent the breadth and span of subjects in our school curriculum. You may rightly ask: What about the unique act of reading music? What about the visual arts – such as 'reading' paintings and sculptures, alongside the conventional reading of their explanatory summaries? These are important questions that I hope the content in this book can prompt further interest, dialogue and action from teachers, without addressing them specifically.

I end the chapter with a clarion call to all teachers to engage in dialogue about their pupils' reading within their subject communities and with bona fide subject experts. Also, importantly, we need to reach across any notional barriers between different school phases – so that we truly draw upon our collective expertise.

> ## IN SHORT …
>
> - It is important to view academic reading through a subject-specific lens in all phases of schooling. By paying attention to the specialised ways of reading in each subject discipline – part of what is termed 'disciplinary literacy' – we can best support our pupils to use subject-specific reading strategies alongside useful general reading strategies.
> - A general reading strategy like rereading is usually applicable in every area of the school curriculum, but it may require specific attention in mathematics to ensure dense word problems are read successfully.
> - We can explicitly teach the language features and reading strategies that relate to the specialised and subject-specific texts of school, such as textbooks, and other informational texts that are typically unique to reading in school contexts.
> - Subject disciplines have their own ways of reading. For example, reading like a historian can include reading strategies like 'sourcing', 'contextualising' and 'corroborating' that are uniquely applicable to reading texts in history.

Notes

1 Woolf, V. (1927). *To the lighthouse*. Oxford: Oxford University Press, p. 13.
2 The Geographical Association (n.d.). Coasts lesson plans: Look at it this way lesson 8. Retrieved from www.geography.org.uk/download/ga_hydrologycoastsl8informationsheet8.pdf.
3 O'Brien, D. G., Moje, E. B., & Stewart, R. A. (2001). Exploring the context of secondary literacy: Literacy in people's

everyday school lives. In E. B. Moje & D. G. O'Brien (Eds.), *Constructions of literacy: Studies of teaching and learning in and out of secondary classrooms* (pp. 27–48). Mahwah, NJ: Lawrence Erlbaum Associates.

4 Education Endowment Foundation (2019). *Improving literacy in secondary schools.* London: Education Endowment Foundation; Shanahan, T., & Shanahan, C. (2012). What is disciplinary literacy and why does it matter? *Topics in Language Disorders, 32*(1), 7–18. doi:10.1097/TLD.0b013e318244557a.

5 Moje, E. B. (2008). Foregrounding the disciplines in secondary literacy teaching and learning: A call for change. *Journal of Adolescent and Adult Literacy, 52*(2), 96–107. doi:10.1598/JAAL.52.2.1

6 Fang, Z., & Schleppegrell, M. J. (2010). Disciplinary literacies across content areas: Supporting secondary reading through functional language analysis. *Journal of Adolescent & Adult Literacy, 53*(7), 587–597. doi:10.1598/JAAL.53.7.6.

7 Meyer, J. B. F. (2003). Text coherence and readability. *Topics in Language Disorders, 23*(3), 204–224. doi:10.1097 / 00011363-200307000-00007.

8 McCormick, S., & Zutell, J. (2015). *Instructing students who have literacy problems* (7th ed.). Boston, MA: Allyn & Bacon.

9 Meyer, J. B. F. (1985). Prose analysis: Purposes, procedures, and problems. In B. K. Britten & J. B. Black (Eds.), *Understanding expository text: A theoretical and practical handbook for analyzing explanatory text* (pp. 11–64). Hillsdale, NJ: Lawrence Erlbaum Associates.

10 Westbrook, J., Sutherland, J., Oakhill, J. V., & Sullivan, S. (2018). 'Just reading': The impact of a faster pace of reading narratives on the comprehension of poorer adolescent readers in English classrooms. *Literacy, 53*(2), 60–68.

11 Jenner, T. (2019). Making reading routine: Helping KS3 pupils to become regular readers of historical scholarship. *Teaching History, 174,* 42–48.

12 Ibid.

13 Counsell, C. (2018). *Senior curriculum leadership 1: The indirect manifestation of knowledge: (A) curriculum as narrative.* Retrieved from https://thedignityofthethingblog.wordpress.com.

14 You can find the list here: https://bit.ly/30olwsp.

15 Lemov, D. (2016). *Reading reconsidered: A practical guide to rigorous literacy instruction.* San Francisco, CA: Jossey-Bass.

16 Bergman, J. (2012). *Hitler and the Nazi Darwinian worldview: How the Nazi eugenic crusade for a superior race caused the greatest Holocaust in world history.* Ontario, Canada: Joshua Press.

17 Camden, B. (2017). Single textbook approved for maths mastery teaching. *Schools Week,* 21 July. Retrieved from https://schoolsweek.co.uk/single-textbook-approved-for-maths-mastery-teaching.

18 Dunlosky, J., & Rawson, K. A. (2012). Overconfidence produces underachievement: Inaccurate self-evaluations undermine students' learning and retention. *Learning and Instruction, 22,* 271–280. Retrieved from https://pdfs.semanticscholar.org/bobb/624eb91d713137f7a8a2a93952cf72750f29.pdf.

19 Ibid.

20 Crawford, H. (2017). *Oxford international primary history: Workbook 2.* Oxford: Oxford University Press.

21 Siebert, D., & Draper, R. J. (2008). Why content-area literacy messages do not speak to mathematics teachers: A critical content analysis. *Literacy Research and Instruction, 47*(4), 229–245. doi:10.1080/19388070802300314.

22 Lindgren, W., Roberts, G., & Sankey, A. (1999). *Introduction to mathematical thinking.* Retrieved from www.tec.iup.edu/mhogue/literary_ review.html, p. 16.

23 Schell, V. (1982). Learning partners: Reading and mathematics. *The Reading Teacher, 35*(5), 544–548, at p. 544.

24 Panchyshyn, R., & Monroe, E. E. (1992). Vocabulary considerations in mathematics instruction. Paper presented at the Fourteenth World Congress on Reading, Maui, Hl.

25 Schwidt-Wiegard, F., Kohnert, A., & Glowalla, U. (2010). A closer look at split visual attention in system- and self-paced instruction in multimedia learning. *Learning and Instruction, 20*(2), 100–110.

26 Fuentes, P. (1998). Reading comprehension in mathematics. *Clearing House, 72*(2), 81–88. doi:10.1080/00098659809599602.

27 Thompson, D. R., & Rubenstein, R. N. (2000). Learning mathematics vocabulary: Potential pitfalls and instructional strategies. *The Mathematics Teacher, 93*(7), 568–574.

28 Counsell, C. (2004). *History in practice: History and literacy in Y7 – building the lesson around the text.* London: Hodder Murray.

29 Wineburg, S. S. (1991). Historical problem solving: A study of the cognitive processes used in the evaluation of documentary and pictorial evidence. *Journal of Educational Psychology, 83*(1), 73–87. doi:10.1037/0022-0663.83.1.73.

30 Foster, R. (2013). The more things change, the more they stay the same: Developing students' thinking about change and continuity. *Teaching History, 151,* 8–17.

31 Rosenblatt, L. M. (1960). Literature: The reader's role. *English Journal, 49*(5), 304–310, 315–316. Retrieved from http://links.jstor.org/sici?sici=00138274%28196005%2949%3A5%3C304%3ALTRR%3E2.0.CO%3B2-3.

32 Protherough, R. (1983). *Developing a response to fiction.* Milton Keynes, UK: Open University.

33 Eagleton, T. (2014). *How to read literature.* New Haven, CT: Yale University Press.

34 Reynolds, T., & Rush, L. S. (2017). Experts and novices reading literature: An analysis of disciplinary literacy in English language arts. *Literacy Research and Instruction, 56*(3), 199–216. doi:10.1080/19388071.2017.1299820.

35 Booker, C. (2004). *Seven basic plots: Why we tell stories.* New York, NY: Continuum Books.

36 Conti, G. (2016). Eleven low-preparation/high-impact tips for enhancing reading tasks. Retrieved from https://bit.ly/2KUPjft.

37 Meschyan, G., & Hernandez, A. (2002). Is native-language decoding skill related to second-language learning? *Journal of Educational Psychology, 94*(1), 14–22.

38 Woore, R., Graham, S., Porter, A., Courtney, L., & Savory, C. (2018). Foreign language education unlocking reading (FLEUR): A study into the teaching of reading to beginner learners of French in secondary school. Retrieved from https://bit.ly/2Qc7Mcg.

39 Ibid.

7 Practical strategies for closing the reading gap

Where do we start when it comes to developing our pupils as readers? The act of reading infiltrates all aspects of learning – in the classroom and at home – and teachers, and pupils, are making countless decisions about reading each day.

Clearly, reading matters and teacher knowledge of reading is essential. And so, it makes sense to begin focusing upon how we create a culture where reading is a priority for everybody. A culture defined by privileging reading, enjoying reading, sharing reading, better understanding reading and doing shedloads of it at every available opportunity.

In 2018, England lost another 130 libraries,[1] cutting at the roots of the very reading culture of our nation. As a mere one in eight disadvantaged pupils own a book, the onus on schools to close the reading gap becomes more pressing and yet more challenging.

School libraries may be on the wane too. Recent survey research by the 'Great Schools Libraries' campaign states that schools with a higher proportion of pupils from disadvantaged backgrounds are "more than twice as likely not to have access to a designated library space."[2] With such factors at play, the reading rich are likely to get richer and the reading poor will get poorer.

Access to books at home matters;[3] access to books in school matters. Access to books matters to interest in books;[4] interest in books matters to sustained practice in reading; sustained practice matters to skill building; skill building matters to engaging with and understanding the academic curriculum. Each link in this chain is vulnerable and needs attending to by teachers.

We therefore need an array of practical approaches, coordinated and developed across school, if we are to help every pupil flourish.

Practical strategies for … creating a whole-school reading culture

- **Love thy library**. Though financial times may be hard, our prioritisation of school funding speaks louder than words. The state of our school library may very well prove the canary in the coal mine for our school reading culture. A trained librarian can be vital in curating the best available fiction and non-fiction, supporting research and aiding teachers to reach beyond the narrow parameters of the taught curriculum. There needs to be joined-up thinking and integration between curriculum development and library use though; otherwise we may not maximise reading development. We should consider:
  1. How many times do we visit the library as part of classroom instruction? Is it an integrated part of curriculum development?
  2. How often do we model and support the selection of reading material?

3. How well do we use library borrowing data and the library space to support struggling readers?
4. How do classroom mini-libraries connect to the main school library?

- **Teachers as readers.** We need to signal that reading is fundamental to successful learning. As such, we need teachers to role model being readers. Though the majority of primary school teachers may read for pleasure, knowledge of children's fiction is invariably weak.[5] It is unlikely that knowledge of high-quality informational texts is any better. And so, we must support teachers to develop their knowledge of the sources of wider reading (a proactive librarian can play this role), as well as modelling our own reading for pleasure and reading for scholarship. Remember, how can we teach pupils to read like a historian if they never actually read what historians write?

- **Reading responsibilities.** We shouldn't shift the seeming burden of reading on to any individual or a harried literacy coordinator. An effective reading culture is prioritised by every leader (particularly the headteacher and executive leadership). Effective curriculum integration requires subject experts contributing and collaborating. Of course, this requires planning and time. If it doesn't feature on the school development plan, it isn't likely to get done. We should ask, who are our team of 'reading ringleaders'?

- **Prolonged promotion of reading.** One-off events like 'World Book Day' can be fun but they too often fail to sustain a reading culture. We instead need daily habits and coordinated plans. Some high-profile events can sustain interest. 'Project 500' is a good example.[6] Named after the library's Dewey Decimal system for science, this project promotes the reading of science books in primary school. It can be integrated with the curriculum and more specifically challenges pupils' misnomers about reading informational texts in particular.[7] We need to sustain reading. Year 6 teacher, Sadie Phillips, has produced a really helpful 'literacy calendar' that charts many of the reading related events throughout the school year.[8]

● **Helping parents to turn the page.** We can recognise the integral importance of the home environment for fostering reading, but parental engagement is a challenge for schools.[9] To make supporting reading accessible for every parent, simple models can be communicated by schools, such as the PEER model:

Prompt the child to say something about the book.

Evaluate their response.

Expand their response by rephrasing or adding information to it.

Repeat the prompt to help them learn from the expansion.[10]

Providing parents with age- and stage-related reading recommendations can also cut to the chase of supporting their children, with websites like https://schoolreadinglist. co.uk offering a comprehensive array of age-related reading.

Practical strategies for ... promoting reading for pleasure and purpose

● **Going beyond 'just books'.** Pupils who read for pleasure identify themselves as readers. Unfortunately, some pupils don't view themselves as 'readers' if they read graphic novels, websites and similar, as they are not deemed 'traditional' books.[11] We should quash this misnomer. Websites like BBC Newsround[12] for younger pupils can be supplemented with lots of magazines and newspapers.[13]

- **'Hard, harder, hardest'**. Whether it is a teacher, a librarian or a parent, we need to ensure that supporting pupils to make good reading choices is something that we do consistently and perhaps for longer than we assume. By offering 'bounded choice' – that is to say, options between reading choices we have selected for pupils – we can support their choice, which is particularly necessary for weaker readers. We can also support weaker readers to pick appropriate reads by taking the stigma away from texts labelled 'easy readers' and similar, replacing them with headings of 'hard, harder, hardest'.[14]

- **Going for goals**. Remember those thieves and home buyers reading with a role and a goal in Chapter 4? Such targeted reading boosts comprehension and memory. And so, the most powerful word we may ever use in our classroom is a simple one: *why*. Asking '*why* am I reading this?' brings a degree of self-control and metacognitive awareness that is important. Simply labelling the goal of reading can help, such as using the acronym REAL:

  Retrieve: reading to retrieve specific information, to answer a question etc.

  Enjoy: reading simply for enjoyment and appreciation.

  Analyse: reading to analyse meaning and dig into layers of meaning.

  Link: reading to connect and/or corroborate ideas and sources, or to consolidate understanding.

Alternatively, beginning a topic with a 'big question' can initiate an enquiry and get pupils cohering what they know, while stimulating their interest in what they are about to read.

- **Monitoring motivation**. Pupils read, or not, for multiple reasons. Of course, the more reading we can support the better. First then, we need to know our pupils' motivations for reading. The 'motivations for reading questionnaire' (MRQ)[15] is a very useful tool to discern what drives their reading.[16] We know that motivation is mediated by how interested our pupils are in what they read (even when it is a very difficult text to read[17]), so connecting reading to their interests really does matter.

Practical strategies for … effective whole-class reading

It is a rare school day when a teacher does not make a choice about how they read with their class. In fact, it is such a common aspect of a teacher's practice, that we can take such decisions without thinking very hard. How can we then make informed choices about how we read with pupils in our classrooms?

We can start by defining different approaches and critic-ally appraising their impact. The following table explores some of the potential benefits and limitations of common approaches to reading.

Clearly, what makes for effective whole-class reading will depend upon the goal of reading, what is being read, as well as the reading ability of pupils.

For example, a year 4 teacher seeking to introduce a challenging informational text for the new topic of climate change, with challenging vocabulary and lengthy sen-tence structures, may likely deem 'teacher-led whole-class reading' necessary in order to ensure the focus is on com-prehension. After reading multiple texts on the same topic, the teacher may then seek to deploy paired reading, to shift the emphasis on to reading practice and developing fluency. 'Paired reading' here could allow for multiple texts to be read at once. The teacher could circulate and monitor for both fluency and comprehension.

Conversely, in a year 10 GCSE French class, the teacher could initiate 'choral reading' to consolidate fluency, pronunciation and familiarity with important vocabulary items for a travel and tourism topic. This could be followed by 'repeated reading', honing fluency further. Finally, 'individual, silent reading', aligned with comprehension questions, could consolidate understanding of the topic, while offering feedback to the teacher on individual responses.

The book or text being read matters to the selection of reading approach. We can apply a familiar 'Goldilocks principle' to this matter. We often select overtly difficult reading texts in the classroom, at pupils' 'frustration level',[18] to push the boundaries of their knowledge. It is invariably supported by teacher-led reading. Alternatively, for homework and similar, we select texts that are reckoned to be more accessible (remember the 'ready reckoner' from Chapter 5?), though still a challenge, for independent silent reading.

	Description of reading approach	Potential benefits	Potential limitations
Teacher-led whole-class reading	The teacher reads with the appropriate degree of fluency (pace, expression, stress and intonation) Typically,	The teacher models fluent, expert reading The teacher can plan to concisely explain vocabulary, ask questions, or offer	Pupils do not gain the opportunity to develop their own reading skill or fluency explicitly Pupils *could* be prone to distraction and passivity

	Description of reading approach	Potential benefits	Potential limitations
	explanations and questions are interspersed during reading, alongside checking vocabulary and monitoring interest etc.	clarifications, during the act of reading The teacher can more specifically control the task	Less-skilled readers may struggle to follow the text and listen to the reading simultaneously
Whole-class reading: pupils selected to read individually in 'round-robin' style	The teacher selects individuals to read (this can be at random, or with individuals selected – which could significantly influence the impact of the approach)	Pupils practise their reading skill Teachers can assess pupils' reading skill and fluency The teacher can more specifically control the task, selecting individuals, posing questions, etc.	Pupils do not gain the opportunity to hear the fluent, expert reading of the teacher Some pupils may feel inhibited regarding reading in front of their peers, hampering their performance and fluency Pupils are not exposed to an amount of practice that would likely enhance their reading skill[a]
Choral reading	With an appropriate passage from a text, the teacher and pupils read in unison Alternatively, the 'antiphon' approach – drawing upon religious	Pupils practise their reading skill Pupils can develop an awareness of reading with the appropriate pace and intonation	Some pupils may feel inhibited to read in this manner in front of their peers, limiting their practice

(*continued*)

Practical strategies

	Description of reading approach	Potential benefits	Potential limitations
	readings – calls for the class to be divided into two or more groups, with each group being responsible for different parts of the text	Less-skilled pupils can develop confidence and fluency, perhaps less inhibited by reading along within a group	Pupils *could* be prone to distraction and passivity during such a group activity, not really reading with the group A focus upon the reading performance *may* prove a distraction from attempts at comprehension
Paired reading	Pupils are arranged into pairs and read to one another. This can be in a fashion that alternates, paragraph by paragraph or page by page	Pupils practise their reading skill Less-skilled pupils can develop confidence and fluency Pupils are assigned clear roles and goals within their reading. There is a shared responsibility The teacher can assess pupils' reading skill and fluency	Pupils do not gain the opportunity to hear the fluent, expert reading of the teacher Pupils *could* be prone to distraction during such a group activity A focus upon their peer's reading performance *may* prove a distraction from attempts at comprehension
Repeated reading	Repeated reading is used with very young children and with mature pupils alike as a way to consolidate	Pupils practise their reading skill There is some evidence that repeated reading can enhance	Pupils do not gain the opportunity to hear the fluent, expert reading of the teacher

Description of reading approach	Potential benefits	Potential limitations
	comprehension Rereading is often guided e.g. a second read to explicitly identify evidence for a causal argument in geography	comprehension (especially if modelled first by a teacher or exemplary audio)[b] Less-skilled pupils can develop confidence and fluency Teachers can assess pupils' reading skill and fluency	Pupils *could* be prone to distraction and passivity, as they do not understand the value of repeated practice This strategy requires more curriculum time, which may or may not compromise curriculum planning Some pupils may lack the strategies to learn from rereading, e.g. scanning for specific information on a repeated read, etc.
Individual, silent reading	Pupils read individually and independently	Pupils practise their reading skill Less-skilled pupils can develop confidence and fluency, without interacting with their peers	Pupils do not gain the opportunity to hear the fluent, expert reading of the teacher For less fluent readers, independent reading is likely to be highly challenging

(*continued*)

Description of reading approach	Potential benefits	Potential limitations
	The teacher may be better able to assess pupils' reading skill and fluency on an individual basis	Some pupils may lack the strategies to monitor their comprehension, e.g. rereading or scanning for specific information Pupils *could* be prone to distraction and passivity

a Shanahan, T. (2019). Is round-robin reading really that bad? Retrieved from www.shanahanonliteracy.com/blog/is-round-robin-reading-really-that-bad.

b Chard D. J., Vaughn, S., & Tyler, B. -J. (2002). A synthesis of research on effective interventions for building reading fluency with elementary students with learning disabilities. *Journal of Learning Disabilities, 35*(5), 386–406.

There are many common approaches to developing independent reading in English schools. Some of the list of acronyms to describe such practices include the following:

- **DEAR** (drop everything and read)[19]
- **SSR** (sustained silent reading)
- **ERIC** (everybody reads in class)
- **RRR** (register, read, respond)[20]
- **FUR** (free uninterrupted reading)

Based on this plethora of acronyms, such approaches to in-school independent reading are widespread, but they can also prove very different in nature. For example, 'register, read, respond' can be more orientated around collectively reading short informational texts in registration/form time, with explicit comprehension questions; whereas 'free uninterrupted reading' assumes pupil choice, with limited scope for comprehension questions, if such questions are attended to at all.

We should critically appraise such important choices with our precious curriculum time. The research evidence that attends sustained silent reading can prove variable in its impact on our pupils' reading: "While silent reading might have other positive outcomes, such as providing a structured start to the school day, overall evaluations of silent reading programmes have shown inconsistent effects on student outcomes and motivation."[21] That is not to say sustained silent reading could not form a valuable part of a whole-school reading culture – it may provide a great vehicle for developing our pupils as readers – but we should ask questions as to our goals and the support factors that pupils need to utilise this time well. We should consider:

- How are pupils going about selecting texts to read?
- Should we provide explicit support to aid pupils' text choices (or only for weaker readers)?
- Should we monitor comprehension as pupils read, or pose questions after they have read to explicitly promote comprehension monitoring?
- How can we support our weakest readers during this reading time (e.g. provide small-group or one-to-one support)?
- Should we explicitly provide specific reading strategies during this reading time?
- What whole-class reading strategies could best support this reading time (e.g. paired reading)?
- Should this reading time be synchronised with curriculum development (e.g. reading informational

and fiction texts focused upon a specific topic being studied)?

- How do we monitor the ongoing impact of sustained silent reading on our pupils' reading motivation and ability?

We then come to the subject-specific differences of making effective whole-class reading approaches work. Sometimes such decisions are made simply due to teacher habit, or familiarity with certain approaches. In recent research focused on the secondary English classroom, there is the suggestion that reading texts at a faster pace – even complex, extended novels – can help the comprehension of weaker readers over a slower step-by-step approach that involves a lot of elaborate activities.[22] Does this 'just read to them' approach translate to reading a chapter on diseases in biology? It is unlikely. And so, decisions that attend disciplinary reading need to be explored and teacher judgement informed by a deep knowledge of reading.

Practical strategies for … promoting reading fluency

- **Repeated reading**. The strategy of repeated reading is a well-practised method to develop fluency, particularly if the rereading is undertaken after a good reader role model, and/or is undertaken one to one with a teacher or teaching assistant. Research suggests that pupils should be given feedback on word errors[23] (e.g. if a pupil hesitates for three seconds, provide the word and have the pupil repeat it); otherwise the repeated reading could in fact do little but practise mistakes until they become a habit.
- **Reading talk**. This teacher-led approach is another one-to-one reading method with struggling pupils that sees

the expert reader read a passage, quickly followed by the pupil. Then there is feedback on dialogue on how 'natural' and 'talk-like' the reading appeared, alongside the pace, phrasing, smoothness, expression and volume (remember the 'multidimensional fluency scale' from Chapter 3?).

- **Echo reading**. Another variation involves the teachers modelling a short passage of reading to offer the pupil expert exemplification. The pupil then 'echoes' by reading the same passage.
- **Segmenting sentences**.[24] Many pupils who lack fluency don't exercise the subtle cues offered by an author, such as using punctuation within sentences to segment words, or noticing the phrases that are meant to be read as a unit, rather than separate words. Some quick one-to-one reading with a pupil could focus on segmenting the sentence into meaningful phrases and paying attention to the patterns and punctuation within the sentences.
- **Read, record**. Recording pupils' reading, then playing it back, alongside a dialogue offers another method for careful reflection. With such recordings, you can be really precise and replay errors and suggest when words could be read better as phrases, etc. Pupils doing this individually first can offer a safe approach to practising their reading.
- **From me to you**. Pupils can be directed to work in pairs to read alternate sentences of a passage, or to repeat the sentences of one another. This can be followed by critical reflection ('who said it best and why?) and corrective feedback.
- **Peer tutoring**.[25] This common strategy is usually structured across age groups. Often undertaken outside of the classroom, it can involve stronger reading peers listening to younger pupils and offering corrective

feedback. To maximise this strategy it is likely that the tutors are trained in the approaches (indeed, they may benefit as much from taking part as the tutees).

Practical strategies for ... developing strategic readers

- **'3, 2, 1'.** Strategic readers are constantly questioning, evaluating and connecting what they read. With this strategy, the pupil is encouraged to generate *three* essential points to consider, connect and remember; *two* key vocabulary items to know, use and remember; and finally, *one* big idea to understand, explain and remember. In doing so, they summarise and distil their understanding.
- **Section summaries.** Our pupils don't always do what we would expect of a reader. Expert readers routinely pause and think, and summarise in their mind or in their notes the salient points of what they have read. The issue is the more you know, the freer you are to slow, stop and connect. For novice readers, we train them into the routine strategy of stopping, puzzling and deciphering patterns. After a chapter, or a passage of extended text, we get pupils to summarise with a single topic sentence, followed by a maximum of three bullet points, ending with: 'I need to remember ...'
- **Six-word summaries.** Another strategy to home in on summarising what has been read is the tricky distillation into a mere six words. For example, Shakespeare's Hamlet is 'Grieving tragic hero; inaction, death, catharsis'. Like the rhyme to remember Henry VIII's wives' bleak fate ('divorced, beheaded, died, divorced, beheaded, survived'), the summary can be a handy memory aid too.

- 'Accountable talk'[26] and reading routines. High-quality discussion, made routine and well structured, strengthens reading comprehension.[27] Simple sentence openers[28] can be made routine and ensure that pupils strategically elaborate what they know:

  What do you think about …?
  How do you know that?
  What is your evidence?
  What questions do you have about …?
  How would you summarise your understanding of …?

By preparing responses in pairs before engaging talk with the teacher, pupils can better formulate their responses, thereby generating high-quality whole-class dialogue.

- **Explain yourself**. The simple act of explaining your thinking (self-explanation) – otherwise known as 'think alouds' – can have a significant impact on your understanding. It supports pupils to construct the all-important mental model of what they have read. It just may need some structured prompt questions, such as parameters of time (e.g. 'just a minute'), the requirement to use clear discourse markers (e.g. first … second … furthermore … in contrast … in conclusion), and the explicit expectation to go beyond paraphrasing and to generate new ideas.
- **The big question**. Building a mental model of what has been read can begin by asking a big question to encourage pupils to seek coherence in what they read and to make connections. In food technology, asking 'how important is food to the environment?' triggers pupils' background knowledge, but it crucially primes

them to then cohere related questions and issues, such as the sustainability of food sources, food wastage and more. It is a simple strategy that can have a profound impact on increasing motivation to read and making our pupils more strategic readers.

- **'Only connect'**. Aidan Chambers stated that when we read "we constantly look for connectedness, for patterns of relationship between one thing and another".[29] As pupils become more strategic, this connection making becomes seemingly 'natural'. We can foster it by repeatedly asking 'how does this connect to what we know?' For example, in religious education, if we are reading about the ethics of Buddhism, we can ask 'how does this connect to what we know about the ethics of Christianity?' A verbal shorthand response to pupils then can be 'connect'. With a little training, this can initiate rich inferences and connections from pupils in classroom dialogue.
- **Study group**. A useful method to vary the approach to reading is to use the collaborative strategy of reading in a 'study group'. It can allow for the reading of more extended texts, as the teacher can allocate different sections of a passage to be read by individuals. For example, in computer science, small groups of pupils can be given a range of problems to read. Then their respective solutions can be read and critically appraised by one another, before being edited and agreed upon. In A-level politics, when given a political manifesto, pupils can be allocated sections with page numbers, before then coming together to summarise their section and share insights.
- **GASE (gist, analysis, synthesis, elaboration)**. Remember the scholars from the Middle Ages in Chapter 2? They read sacred texts repeatedly, with a

first, second and third read. Such close reading still defines scholarly reading today. We can guide this with the step-by-step GASE method. The first read ascertains the **gist** of the text; the second read poses a deeper **analysis**, ensuring understanding and making inferences; with the third read **synthesising** the main ideas, by summarising the text and connecting it to other ideas, topics or texts; finally, we ask pupils to **elaborate** on ideas emerging from the text and connecting it to other reading. For example, when reading a poem in year 4, we may first get the gist and check we understand the words and imagery. Then we analyse the patterns of imagery and the ideas and emotions presented by the poet. After that, pupils synthesise the main ideas and poetic style. Finally, pupils connect the poem to other poems, genres and literary themes.

Practical strategies for … promoting quality questioning

Promoting high-quality questioning in the classroom may just prove the most important way to promote the strategic thinking that improves our pupils' reading. By promoting, structuring and modelling questions relentlessly, and integrating them into classroom reading routines, we help pupils at every stage of reading: before, during and after their reading.

- **Question categorisation.** It is helpful for teachers to first consider what types of questions will support reading or elicit the types of inferences we want our pupils to make about what they read. Angelo Cardiello[30] offers a very handy categorisation of question types, shown in the following table.

Practical strategies

Question type	Definition	Examples
Memory questions	Who, what, when and where? Naming and defining questions	What is gravity? Who invented the light bulb? Where was the Battle of Trafalgar fought?
Convergent thinking questions	Why, how and in what way? Questions that explain and convey relationships/cause and effect, etc.	What are the causes of climate change? How and why do volcanoes erupt? How is apartheid related to racism in 1960s America?
Divergent thinking	Imagine, predict, if ... then ... Questions that hypothesise, predict and infer	What future predictions can you make about the impact of global temperatures? What are the reasons for Hamlet's depressed mental state? How might life in India be different if Gandhi's protest against Britain's control of salt had not happened?
Evaluative thinking	Judge, justify your position ... Questions that develop arguments and defend and justify points	Should drugs be legalised? Why do people choose to live in urban areas? How might life in England be different if Nazi Germany won World War II?

We can utilise such categories to model, record and monitor different question types as pupils read tricky academic texts across a range of subject disciplines.

- **Questioning the author**. Literacy experts Isabel Beck and Margaret McKeown have devised a model to ask high-quality questions that specifically promotes close-reading engagement from our pupils.[31] The approach is about asking text-specific questions that get pupils elaborating on the aims of the author, e.g. Why do you think the author uses the word choice ...? What does the author want to convey about the difficulties of ...? With some teacher-collaborative planning, questioning the author sequences could be developed for key texts being read in our classrooms. Very helpfully, Beck and McKeown outline three key steps to deploy this method in a lesson:
  1. **Identify major aspects of the text to understand** – as well as potential misconceptions that are likely to arise.
  2. **Segment and chunk the text**. Teachers should deliberately break down the text so that the teacher can regularly check understanding.
  3. **Develop queries to consolidate understanding**. For example, before reading a text, identify stopping points and question prompts to initiate discussion.
- **Self-questioning**. Self-questioning is a robust way to develop successful, strategic readers.[32] Effectively, it is about the continual promotion of active reading and the modelling of the questions that expert readers can ask habitually, and near instantaneously, as they read. Self-questioning can be supported by teacher modelling aloud during the reading process, before then directly posing those questions to pupils. Over time, such questions can become internalised by our pupils. We can use who, what, when, where and why prompts, or Cardiello's question categories as a structure.
- **The power of why**. One way to ensure that pupils engage deeply with what they have read is to ask

'why' questions that ensure pupils probe their back-ground knowledge, make connections and elaborative inferences. Even incorrect answers to 'why' questions can enhance pupils' learning.[33] Why questions that pre-cede reading can help pupils to better focus upon the role and goal of their reading.

- **Socratic circles.** This age-old strategy offers a structured group model to then promote quality questioning and dia-logue. The model – including an 'inner circle' discussing, with an 'outer circle' listening and formulating questions – offers space to develop well-crafted questions. This online resource offers a clear structure for developing Socratic circles based around reading texts.[34]

Practical strategies for … writing to support reading

Reading and writing are literacy processes that are inex-tricably linked. It is clear that asking pupils to write about what they read can improve reading comprehension and so we should teach both together.[35]

- **List, group, label**. This well-established strategy[36] supports pupils to record and organise their understanding of key vocabulary and information from a text. First, select a topic/theme that has emerged, or will emerge, in what is being read. Then get pupils to list as many words and ideas related to that topic/ theme. Then work to cluster the words and ideas into subcategories. Then decide on the best labels for these clusters. This strategy can organise prior knowledge, generate disciplined discussion and prime pupils to read strategically.
- **Going global**. Remember 'global inferences' from Chapter 4? They are the inferences pupils make as they

connect words, sentences and ideas to the 'global' structure of the whole text. Pupils can gain from this process being modelled explicitly by the teacher before then internalising the strategy. Simply select a word, phrase, sentence, passage or section – invoke the globe symbol and then write about the wider connections from the micro example identified to the macro structure of the text. For example, when reading a geographical text, a passage exploring fires in the Amazon can be connected to wider environmental, economic and political debates.

- **Expert checklists**. Checklists can be derided by some as a simplistic way to distil writing. However, when we consider how experts such as surgeons and fighter pilots – and of course teachers – can gain from utilising a humble checklist, we should consider using this tool for reading too. When reading a text, we can read with disciplinary expertise by recording the important information from a text using an expert checklist. For example, a handy prompt for a historian reading a chapter in a book, could be to have a checklist to remember to 'corroborate' sources or to 'contextualise' the evidence.

- **Summarising with subheadings**.[37] Summarising comes in many forms and is an established strategy for improving reading comprehension.[38] By first modelling selecting key information and removing trivial information, such as in the chapter of a physical education GCSE textbook, we can create concise summaries, with appropriate subheadings identified. Ultimately, pupils distil the essentials of what they have read, thereby thinking hard about the text and making it easier to be remembered.

- **Note-taking: 'select, summarise, question'**. Note-taking is widely accepted and practised as a method of processing, organising and recording our thinking about what we read.[39] Too often though, such note-taking isn't consistently modelled or structured and so even the skilled readers don't maximise the benefits of note-taking. We should explicitly model note-taking, such as the 'Cornell Method', etc. Including summary questions in our notes can also offer useful tools for when we return to our notes.

Practical strategies for ... vocabulary instruction to support reading

Vocabulary knowledge is indisputably essential for reading success. Vocabulary instruction then should play an important part in our approach to teaching reading. Here are just a few strategies that help to highlight the importance of vocabulary before, during and after reading.

- **Talk, try, test**. Multiple exposures to new academic vocabulary can be targeted and cumulative through the school curriculum. By structuring multiple exposures to important words in texts, we help secure reading comprehension. 'Talk, try, test' organises repeated exposures with key vocabulary (handy for curriculum planning):
  Exposure 1: Teacher/pupils *talk* about the word.
  Exposure 2: Return to the word, getting pupils to *try* and use it in their talk/writing.
  Exposure 3: *Test* their knowledge of the word.
- **Vocabulary bookmarks**. This simple but effective strategy creates reading bookmarks – used in informational texts and textbooks, as much as fiction – to help record key vocabulary. It is a versatile approach. You can have different headings or colours atop each side of the bookmark, e.g. red for difficult words you need to find out more about, with green representing important vocabulary or words you want to use in your writing,

etc. You could select interesting words, disciplinary vocabulary, confusing words and more.

- **Word webs**. Word webs is simply a form of note-taking involving identifying important vocabulary and creating groupings/categories of related words or ideas in interconnected webs. These graphic representations of important vocabulary can offer a structure to explore word meanings, definitions, as well as memorable word histories and word parts.
- **Idiom identification**. Part of the academic language of reading in school includes a wealth of idioms that for many pupils proves a hidden code they can struggle to decipher. Teachers need to help identify such patterns, so that pupils don't miscomprehend their meaning as they read. For example, idioms like 'cut corners' or 'devil's advocate' can appear even in formal academic texts, so we need to identify them and explore them.

To read much more about the role of vocabulary in reading, read the first book in this series, *Closing the Vocabulary Gap*.

As we consider how useful or interesting different practical strategies may prove, we need to consider the humdrum reality that great new ideas often wilt in the crucible of the classroom. And so, we need to consider how we may select, prioritise and implement a small number of the aforementioned strategies into our existing toolkit of classroom approaches.

Context matters. If we are teaching a year 5 class a new, challenging science topic, such as forces and the theory of gravitation,[40] we need to consider what we read with them (how much do they need to know about Newton?), how we read, as well as how we will foster strategic reading in our pupils.

Notes

1 Cain, S. (2018). Nearly 130 public libraries closed across Britain in the last year. *Guardian*. Retrieved from www.theguardian.com/books/2018/dec/07/nearly-130-public-libraries-closed-across-britain-in-the-last-year.

2 Great School Libraries (2019). *Great school libraries survey findings and update on phase 1.* London: Great School Libraries, p. 5.

3 Evans, M. D. R., Kelly, K., Sikora, J., & Treiman, D. J. (2010). Family scholarly culture and educational success: Books and schooling in 27 nations. *Research in Social Stratification and Mobility, 28*(2), 171–197.

4 Mullis, I. V. S., Martin, M. O., Foy, P., & Hooper, M. (2017). *PIRLS 2016 international results in reading.* Retrieved from http://timssandpirls.bc.edu/pirls2016/international-results.

5 Cremin, T., Mottram, M., Bearne, E., & Goodwin, P. (2008). Exploring teachers' knowledge of children's literature. *Cambridge Journal of Education, 38*(4), 449–464.

6 See https://bit.ly/31XOpWK.

7 Alexander. J., & Jarman, R. (2018). The pleasures of reading non-fiction. *Literacy, 52*(2). https://doi.org/10.1111/lit.12152.

8 See https://bit.ly/2KNGEwA.

9 Education Endowment Foundation (2019). *Working with parents to support children's learning.* London: Education Endowment Foundation.

10 Education Endowment Foundation (2018). *Preparing for literacy: Improving communication, language and literacy in the early years.* London: Education Endowment Foundation.

11 Kolb, C. (2014). *Relationships between discourse, reader identity, and reading self-efficacy in a high school English classroom: A mixed methods, critical ethnographic study.* Minneapolis: University of Minnesota Press.

12 See www.bbc.co.uk/newsround.

13 See the recommendations list via 'The School Reading List' at https://bit.ly/2NtRVnB.

14 Young, N. D. (2017). *From floundering to fluent: Reading and teaching struggling readers.* London: Rowman & Littlefield.

15 Wigfield, A., & Guthrie, J. T. (1997). Relations of children's motivation for reading to the amount and breadth of their reading. *Journal of Educational Psychology, 89,* 420–432.

16 See www.cori.umd.edu/measures/MRQ.pdf.

17 Fulmer, S. M., & Frijters, J. C. (2011). Motivation during an excessively challenging reading task: The buffering role of relative topic interest. *Journal of Experimental Education,* 79(2),185–208. https://doi.org/10.1080/00220973.2010.481503.

18 Brown, L. T., Mohr, K. A. J., Wilcox, B. R., & Barrett, T. S. (2018). The effects of dyad reading and text difficulty on third-graders' reading achievement. *Journal of Educational Research, 111*(5), 541–553. doi:10.1080/00220671.2017.1310711.

19 Gardner, T. (2003). Drop everything, and read! Retrieved from https://eric.ed.gov/?id=ED476414.

20 Developed by Lyndsey Dyer and Alice Visser-Furay. See https://readingforpleasureandprogress.com.

21 Education Endowment Foundation (2019). *Improving literacy in secondary school.* London: Educational Endowment Foundation.

22 Westbrook, J. Sutherland, J., Oakhill, J. V., & Sullivan, S. (2018). 'Just reading': The impact of a faster pace of reading narratives on the comprehension of poorer adolescent readers in English classrooms. *Literacy, 53*(2), 60–68.

23 Therrien, W. J., & Kubina, R. M., Jr. (2006). Developing reading fluency with repeated reading. *Intervention in School and Clinic, 41*(3), 156–160.

24 Stoddard, K., Valcante, G., Sindelar, P., O'Shea, L., & Algozzin, B. (1993). Increasing reading rate and comprehension: The effects of repeated readings, sentence segmentation, and intonation training. *Literacy Research and Instruction,* 32(4), 53–65. doi:10.1080/19388079309558133.

25 Education Endowment Foundation (2019). *Peer tutoring: Toolkit strand.* Retrieved from https://educationendow mentfoundation.org.uk/evidence-summaries/teaching-learning-toolkit/peer-tutoring.

26 Resnick, L., Asterhan, C., & Clarke, S. (2018). *Accountable talk: Instructional dialogue that builds the mind. educational practices series.* International Academy of Education and the International Bureau of Education. Retrieved from

Practical strategies

www.researchgate.net/publication/324830361_Accountable_ Talk_Instructional_dialogue_that_builds_the_mind.

27 Wilkerson, I., Murphy, K., & Binici, S. (2015). Dialogue-intensive pedagogies for promoting reading comprehension: What we know, what we need to know. In L. Resnick, C. Asterhan, & S. Clarke (Eds.), *Socializing intelligence through academic talk and dialogue* (pp. 37–50). Washington, DC: American Educational Research Association.

28 Resnick, L., Asterhan, C., & Clarke, S. (2018). *Accountable talk: Instructional dialogue that builds the mind. educational practices series*. International Academy of Education and the International Bureau of Education. Retrieved from www.researchgate.net/publication/324830361_Accountable_ Talk_Instructional_dialogue_that_builds_the_mind, p. 19.

29 Chambers, A. (1993). *Tell me: Children, reading and talk*. Stroud, UK: Thimble Press, p. 18.

30 Ciardiello, A. V., & Cicchelli, T. (1994). The effects of instructional training models and content knowledge on student questioning in social studies. *Journal of Social Studies Research, 19*, 30–37.

31 Beck, I., & McKeown, M. G. (2002). Questioning the author: Making sense of social studies. *Reading and Writing in the Content Areas, 60*(3), 44–47. Retrieved from www. readingrockets.org/content/pdfs/ASCD_358_1.pdf. See also www.readingrockets.org/strategies/question_the_author.

32 Joseph, L. M., Alber-Morgan, S., Cullen, J., & Rouse, C. (2016). The effects of self-questioning on reading comprehension: A literature review. *Reading & Writing Quarterly, 32*(2), 152–173. doi:10.1080/10573569.2014.891449.

33 Pressley, M., Wood, E., Woloshyn, V. E. Martin, V., King, A., & Menke, D. (1992). Encouraging mindful use of prior knowledge: Attempting to construct explanatory answers facilitates learning. *Educational Psychologist, 21*(1), 91–109.

34 See www.corndancer.com/tunes/tunes_print/soccirc.pdf.

35 Graham, S., Liu, X., Aitken, A., Ng, C., Bartlett, B., Harris, K., & Holzapfel, J. (2017). Effectiveness of literacy programs balancing reading and writing instruction: A meta-analysis. *Reading Research Quarterly, 53*(3), 279–304. doi:10.1002/ rrq.194; Graham, S., & Hebert, M. (2011). Writing to read: A

meta-analysis of the impact of writing and writing instruction on reading. *Harvard Educational Review, 81*(4), 710–744. doi:10.17763/haer.81.4.t2k0m13756113566.

36 Reading Rockets (2019). List-group-label. Retrieved from www.readingrockets.org/strategies/list_group_label.

37 Graham, S., & Hebert, M. A. (2010). *Writing to read: Evidence for how writing can improve reading. A Carnegie Corporation time to act report.* Washington, DC: Alliance for Excellent Education, p. 23.

38 Rinehart, S. D., Stahl, S. A., & Erickson, L. G. (1986). Some effects of summarization training on reading and studying. *Reading Research Quarterly, 21*, 422–438.

39 Graham, S., & Hebert, M. A. (2010). *Writing to read: Evidence for how writing can improve reading. A Carnegie Corporation time to act report.* Washington, DC: Alliance for Excellent Education.

40 Department for Education (2013). *Science programmes of study: Key stages 1 and 2: National curriculum in England.* London: Department for Education.

8 Next steps

Take the time to sit with Rebecca for a moment.

It was in the school library that I sat across from Rebecca. At the end of a long autumn day – for us both – I attempted to spark her into life, nudging her to give her best effort to catch up with her missed reading.

Slumped on the desk, with the only sign of life a habitual tugging on the torn cuffs of her school jumper, Rebecca was unresponsive to my apparent urgency and enthusiasm. "But sir, I hate reading!"

After years in the classroom, hearing this familiar refrain would often spark a well-rehearsed retort. And yet, empathising with Rebecca's truthful and bitter response, I held off replaying the script about the importance of reading and the many doors it can open in our lives.

For Rebecca, "I hate reading" was uttered with a sharp, honest exasperation that is all too common. It was no lazy teen angst. Each day, Rebecca would come to school and suffer countless infinitesimally small losses as she struggled with reading. Every chapter, worksheet, teacher explanation and classroom debate would remind Rebecca of her battle. Each time, she would struggle, question, forget and do so largely hidden from view.

Over time, starved of the pleasure of success, Rebecca's attitude to school, and reading, would harden into prophetic failure. No degree of my enthusiasm could compensate for Rebecca's losses, nor gift her the knowledge to read with the requisite skill that makes reading feel easy, natural or pleasurable.

I saved what felt like a trite script about the importance of reading. Instead, with a quietened class spread across the school library, I began reading to Rebecca. Like reading to my own children at bedtime, she sat with her head perfectly still and began listening.

After a few minutes, Rebecca sat herself up. Her hand momentarily released from gripping her cuff, she opened the book and began to follow along.

The importance of closing the reading gap

Most things teachers do are important but teaching reading – whether that is helping young children sound out their first words or supporting teens to read tricky tomes – is essential.

If pupils like Rebecca can't read fluently, knowledgeably and strategically, we can plan the best, richest curriculum, but they will not access it. With bitter certainty, we also know that those pupils who have no bookshelves to call their own are less likely to close the gap with their peers, in the classroom and beyond.

For the one in four pupils who don't reach the 'expected standard' of reading at the end of primary school, we can make assumptions about both their past struggles and daily failures, while also making gloomy predictions about their future success if they don't speedily improve their reading skill.[1]

Next steps

The hugely successful children's author, Katherine Rundell, stated a timeless truth that "books crowbar the world open for you – every book you read makes your imagination larger."[2] Whether it is fictional worlds expanding our imagination, or informational texts giving us access to a world of powerful knowledge, teachers have it within their power to help prise open those worlds for our pupils.

It is important for every teacher to see reading with new eyes – recognising the challenges, barriers and opportunities it poses for every pupil – alongside its tremendous potential to enrich our lives. As winners of the school game, we can too easily be blind to the issues related to reading or expect other school staff to address the issues. Unconfident about dyslexia or a pupil struggling with comprehension, we can pass along the issue to the special educational needs coordinator (SENCO) or similar.

As shown by this book, our knowledge of reading development, and attendant barriers, can often prove thin, so our ability to address issues and maximise opportunities is compromised. Another crucial reading gap then is teachers' knowledge of reading. It is a gap that proves an issue the world over, from Australia to Accrington.[3] For most of my 15 years in the classroom, my knowledge of how children best read, along with the most effective approaches for instruction, rested upon some personal reading and paltry amounts of teacher-training time devoted to this issue.

We cannot allow reading to be caught and not taught. To make this change, teachers need support. Pupils like Rebecca depend upon it.

For teachers, it is important that they are supported with the requisite time and expertise, so that they better teach reading and inform the many decisions they make in the classroom related to reading each and every day. Only then can we take on the challenge of closing the reading gap.

How do we know we are improving reading?

A vital part of putting our knowledge of reading into action in the classroom is to understand how to best assess reading.

Assessing reading, as shown in the previous chapters, is a challenge. Our attempts at assessment in the classroom are, as Professor Rob Coe describes, the gathering of "multiple inadequate glances" on the matter of reading.[4] Chasing down a rich, varied picture of such 'glances' is the best we can do and an important part of the daily business of the classroom.

We may only be able to take partial, meaningful 'glances' at reading, but we are better served if we understand what aspects of reading to assess and what they can tell us:

Word reading (as addressed in Chapter 3). We can check upon our pupils' phonemic awareness, so important to basic word reading, with diagnostic questions that explore the following:

1. **Phonemic matching**: Can pupils identity words that begin with the same sound, e.g. 'fat' and 'fact'?
2. **Phoneme manipulation**: Can pupils change or move around sounds in a word, e.g. deleting the 'b' sound in 'black' to make 'lack'?
3. **Phoneme blending**: 'Sh – o – p' is blended and pronounced 'shop'.
4. **Phoneme segmentation**: Doing the reverse of blending – breaking down a word into its component sounds, e.g. 'street' becomes 's – t – r – ee – t'.

Reading fluency and **reading-rate assessments** can be undertaken in a matter of minutes, utilising the 'multi-dimensional fluency scale' (see Appendix) and similar. Fluency can prove a bridge between word learning and then comprehension, so it is a very useful glance at reading. A reading-rate assessment can quickly detect issues and anomalies from simply recording words read per minute (WPM).

Alternatively, we can devise manageable assessments such as a 'miscue analysis'.[5] This assessment is a closer analysis of our pupils' reading of a given passage. We can better track both their fluency and their accuracy with this method. Either by recording pupils, or more simply making notes on the text as they read, we can take a fuller glance at their reading ability.

We can use the following categorisation[6] to track the miscues:

Miscue	Symbol	
Omission		Circle words that are omitted during reading
Insertion	∧	A pupil adds a word into the sentence that doesn't appear
Repetition	Underline	Underline words that are repeated in error
Correction	c	Note words that have to be corrected to support reading
Hesitation	/ //	Include a forward slash for small hesitations and a double slash for extended hesitations
Substitution	**PILOT** plot	Write the word the pupil has substituted into the text above the word from the passage

With a closer focus on individual miscues, we can begin to differentiate issues with decoding and vocabulary knowledge, from pauses and struggles with the convoluted structure of some sentences. The number of miscues per 100 words becomes another useful diagnostic tool to monitor over time, akin to the 'ready reckoner' in Chapter 5. We can also note when pupils use desirable reading strategies, such as rereading and self-correction.

Vocabulary knowledge[7] and inference making can be assessed using accessible classroom approaches, such as quizzes and multiple-choice questions, as well as more formal standardised assessments, like the 'British picture vocabulary scale' or the 'Peabody picture vocabulary test'.[8]

Reading comprehension is without doubt complex and challenging to assess and "any attempt to assess reading comprehension is inherently imperfect".[9] And yet, given comprehension is so valuable, gleaning insights is essential work. We can make inferences that alert us to the comprehension of our pupils by asking questions about the text being read. Reading comprehension assessment can be assessed with a simple quiz in the classroom, or in more comprehensive standardised assessments.

If we are building our own reading comprehension quizzes, we have different categories of questions we can deploy:[10]

- **Selected response questions**: questions that offer pupils' optional answers, e.g. multiple-choice questions, closed questions with optional answers, true/false questions.
- **Constructed response questions**: questions that require pupils to wholly construct their answers, e.g. open-ended questions, paragraph written response, essay response.

Both types of question categories have strengths or weaknesses. A teacher may be able to quickly devise a batch of quiz true/false questions, but some answers can then be guessed. Conversely, it may be more complex to generate a good assessment rubric for a 'constructed response' essay, but then pupils have to apply their knowledge in more developed ways, removing issues such as guessing.

Teachers are vital and we can make great intuitive insights into the needs and progress of our pupils' reading comprehension, but sometimes we plainly need a standardised assessment to judge where our pupils stand relative to age-related norms. Happily, there are a range of high-quality standardised reading assessments including:

- **New group reading test (NGRT)**. This detailed assessment includes sentence completion (mainly measuring decoding ability) and passage comprehension. It can be useful broadly for large groups of pupils across a wide range of age groups.
- **Hodder group reading tests**. This is a detailed assessment that includes word level, sentence level and passage analysis. Akin to the NGRT, it can be used with large groups of pupils across age ranges.
- **York assessment of reading comprehension (YARC)**. This assessment has age-appropriate tests, with decoding and comprehension skills assessed, using a range of fiction and informational texts. It is a more specialist one-to-one assessment.
- **The Salford reading test**. This adaptive test involves reading sentences for comprehension and is completed on a one-to-one basis.
- **Diagnostic reading analysis**. This assessment tests reading accuracy, reading fluency/rate and the comprehension of struggling readers between the ages of 7 and 16. This is assessed on a one-to-one basis.

Reading motivation proves a key support factor for helping struggling pupils improve, as it can help determine pupils' will to engage in challenging reading. For weaker readers, motivation is typically dulled, causing a vicious cycle of behaviour. Given the importance of motivation, it is worth giving it the attention offered by assessment. Established reading motivation assessments include the 'Motivations for Reading Questionnaire' (MRQ).[11]

With each assessment we deploy on reading in the classroom, the more informed 'glances' we take of our pupils reading ability. Quickly, we can develop a rich evidence picture that can inform our teaching, our book choices and directions within the school curriculum.

Growing a reading culture and curriculum

Let's return to the image of the empty bookshelf. If book access is such an issue for many pupils, then surely we should move heaven and earth – our planning priorities and the weight of our budget – to flood access to great reading resources for our pupils?

Like many of our school priorities the argument is both urgent and compelling. And yet, we are all too often forced to confront the difficult reality that many innovations for book gifting, culture change and curriculum development fail. Such attempts often don't have the desired impact despite our concerted efforts.

Being immersed in reading, forming reading routines in the school day and at home, alongside engaging in rich talk about what we read are all to be highly prized. But we should be wary of assuming simple solutions will attend what are complex changes to the habits and practices of pupils, parents and teachers. Indeed, 'book gifting' is a well-trodden approach, but finding ingredients of success are harder to come by. First, reading development starts long before the more formal instruction of school,[12] so the die is cast for many pupils early on. Not only that, we may pursue book gifting for individual pupils who are struggling, or who lack the material supports outside of school, but the robust fabric of advantaged homes (full bookshelves, Wi-Fi/technology access, help with homework, tutoring and more) makes closing the reading gap a huge challenge.

Book gifting has been offered as a solution to the reading gap the world over, including familiar national projects in England like 'Bookstart Baby'. In one research trial, called the 'Letterbox Club' (after the lovely package gifted to families) children in care were given a package of books and other learning materials, like stationery, etc. The research revealed little positive impact related to the book gifting beyond the initial pleasure of enjoying the package. The findings did note that they would need to support the parents to utilise the 'gift' to better effect.[13]

Simply giving our pupils, or their families, books won't go all the way to addressing the issue of reading better and being motivated to read more.

Summer reading programmes that attempt to address the 'summer slide' – whereat pupils who don't read can fall behind their peers – have showed some promise. Also, some positive evidence indicates that simply texting parents with reminders, encouragement and suggestions for reading and literacy activities can help the literacy development of our pupils.[14]

Simply sending text messages to parents can help, but it is likely that combining this simple approach with other support factors is going to increase the likelihood parents can engage and support building our pupils' reading habits so key to the reading culture we create in the classroom. In an Education Endowment Foundation project, named the 'Summer Active Reading Programme', there were further positive findings.[15] The project involved free book packs and two summer events. Small gains in reading comprehension were detected. Surprisingly, however, children from more advantaged backgrounds reported increased reading enjoyment, but pupils in receipt of free school meals (FSM) – a proxy for disadvantage – did not.

We should once again be chastened and return to challenging our assumptions about how we best support our pupils, alongside developing a reading culture and curriculum.

Reading access, motivation and reading achievement act in a complex spiral – which can move downwards, like in the case of Rebecca, or upwards. In trying to develop a coordinated approach to developing a reading culture, wedded to reading access, practice and reading ability, we should ask:

- What support factors will be needed to improve access to books, in the classroom, in the school library and at home?
- What training needs do teachers, parents and pupils have to ensure that pupils read more and improve their reading ability (i.e. read more strategically and knowledgeably)?
- As we develop a reading culture and curriculum, what will be "expected, supported and rewarded"?[16]
- How will we assess and evaluate our reading culture, e.g. reading volume, changing reading habits, classroom practice and reading attainment, etc.?

We can follow these questions with a closer attention to the content of our reading curriculum:

- In developing a reading curriculum, what is the balance of fiction and informational texts?
- In developing a reading curriculum, how do we determine a progression of complexity and a coherence of content in our reading choices?

Next steps

- In developing a reading curriculum, how will we come to decisions about text choices, sequences, monitoring progress, etc.?
- In developing a reading curriculum, how do we account for differences in disciplinary reading?

To attend to these questions, we return once more to the necessity of training for school teachers, and school leaders, on different aspects of reading development, alongside how to implement an effective approach to developing reading both in the classroom and in the wider culture and community of the school.

Teachers need the time, training and tools if they are to support all of their pupils to become flourishing readers. Given the tremendous value reading success offers for our pupils, we should invest our efforts in prioritising closing the reading gap.

Whole-school strategies for closing the reading gap

The following two school case studies offer a window into how schools attempt to plan and implement reading across their school. It is a challenge for both primary and secondary schools, in different ways, but there are also common ingredients to consider as we plan to close the reading gap:

Case study 1: reading for pleasure and progress at St Matthew's C of E Primary School – an EEF research school based in Birmingham

Teaching reading matters, but in an area of high deprivation and challenge, becoming expert at teaching reading well is crucial. At St Matthew's, we have committed ourselves to improving our subject knowledge, in teaching reading for pleasure and for progress and we have been determined to uphold the balance between the two. In fact, for us, one cannot exist without the other, so the deliberateness of our approaches to both has been essential to our reading success.

Reading for pleasure is the beating heart of our school. We devote energy and sacrosanct curriculum time to ensuring that, whether it is interactive, solitary or social, this time is done well, every day. Our teachers are specifically trained on the pedagogies that research has proven have the most impact on developing children's love of reading.[17] The one we promote strongly is the importance of becoming, 'a reader who teaches and a teacher who reads'. We have found that in supporting our teachers to model good independent reading practices themselves, they became more determined to nurture their children's independent reading. This was particularly so with regard to deepening and widening their reading preferences.

Our school environment and class reading spaces evoke an atmosphere where reading for pleasure is valued and purposeful. To cement what we feel is our 'moral imperative', we have deliberately had reading for pleasure on our school improvement plan (SIP). This served to hold us to account for our commitment.

Our embedding of reading for pleasure is absolutely matched by our explicit and rigorous approach to teaching the knowledge and skills of reading.[18] Again, we have been led by extensive research and ensured that our teachers are thoroughly trained to teach reading using guided, shared (whole-class) and independent strategies.[19] These are used in our classrooms to teach both language comprehension and word recognition.

Next steps

The approaches for our whole-class reading are based on Doug Lemov's, 'close-reading' strategies. After attending a two-day workshop with Lemov, our teachers were trained to deliver all the aspects outlined in his book, *Reading Reconsidered.*[20] This approach led to a rigour, not only in the teaching of close text examination, but also in the way that we teach vocabulary and its deliberate application across the curriculum.

This has impacted across the curriculum. Through our embedded subject-specific teaching, children are eager to increase their background knowledge, often reading at home and referencing that reading back in lessons. They are also eager to use their vocabulary journals, to record and investigate etymology and morphology, which complements our teaching of Latin.

The impact of this balanced and deliberate approach to the teaching of reading, for both pleasure and progress, has been measured in both attainment outcomes and children's surveys, which state that our children love reading, in all of its forms.

Case study 2: reading the St Mary's literary canon at
St Mary's Catholic Academy – an EEF research school
based in Blackpool

Our approach to reading came in response to it being identified as a whole-school issue. Through careful analysis of attainment and reading-age data, together with discussions with middle leaders, we identified a need for our students to increase the quantity and frequency – and to improve the effectiveness – of their reading.

At St Mary's Catholic Academy, we now take a deliberate and intentional approach to language development, involving combining regular opportunities for reading and explicit vocabulary instruction. We strive to ensure that every pupil can read with fluency and comprehension, as we recognise this is key to successfully unlocking the curriculum.

Rather than simply encouraging students to read more frequently, we took significant measures to ensure that reading time was explicitly set aside in the school day and that students are reading texts that are likely to build their 'cultural capital'.

In order to provide regular opportunities for reading, the timings of the school day were adjusted, and 30 minutes reading time was added to the school timetable on four afternoons each week. During this time, pupils read a carefully chosen selection of books that make up 'St Mary's literary canon'. The challenging texts that make up the canon cover a range of genres, cultures and eras, and offer an exploration of a range of themes and big ideas.

Reading time is delivered by form tutors to mixed-attainment form groups, with extensive staff continuing professional development (CPD) time being used to introduce staff to a range of reading strategies, including teacher-led reading and paired reading. As the reading programme has progressed, CPD time has been used to share best practice around reading routines, with all staff having the opportunity to observe a colleague during reading time.

Staff 'book leads' were appointed to read and resource each literary canon book – producing a knowledge organiser for staff and another for pupils – while they were responsible for leading CPD for form tutors. This CPD, in line with what the evidence suggests, was sustained and iterative and occurred in advance of form tutors reading a book with their form.

The knowledge organisers have a common format. This includes chapter summaries and suggested discussion questions for staff, as well as a vocabulary list and further reading suggestions for pupils. Further reading suggestions are shared with parents via text message, while they also receive a weekly update, detailing which literary canon book their child is reading and a suggested question for discussion with their child.

Early indications are very promising, with GL assessments' 'new group reading test' data showing that two KS3 year groups have shifted from 'in-line with' to 'significantly above the national average' in reading.

— — —

Take some time to consider the essential ingredients of these school approaches. Think about how their school context is similar or different, as well as what support factors are needed to make a positive change happen in our schools.

Few schools are not already addressing reading in some form or another, but the deliberateness of these school case studies is useful to reflect on reading in our own school context.

The power of reading

It would be fitting to end this book extolling the power of reading.

For the past 5,000 years, reading has transformed how we live and offered us the means to live better. The emancipatory power of reading to free the mind, lift the heart and crowbar open future doors promised by school success, is widely understood and, for many, it is a deeply held passion.

We only have to scan our history to recognise the power of reading. In the dark corners of our collective history, it is stories of tyrants, from Caligula burning books by Homer, to Hitler's infamous burning of books and worse on Kristallnacht, and their attempts to censure reading, which remind us that reading can be both liberating and empowering, physically and metaphorically. They also remind us that access to reading can prove vulnerable.

If we are inclined to forget the importance of reading, we can return to the words that begin this book attributed to the former slave, great statesman and writer, Frederick Douglass: "Once you learn to read, you will be forever free."

A story that has struck deep in my consciousness is the deplorable treatment of slaves in America, like Douglass, who attempted to read. One such slave, Doc Daniel Dowdy, from Oklahoma, retold the story of the treatment of his fellow slaves: "The first time you was caught trying to read or write, you was whipped with a cow-hide, the next time with a cat-o-nine tails and the third time they cut the first joint offen your forefinger."[21] Not only that, many white slave masters eagerly hanged any black slave caught trying to teach another to read.

Dwell on that callous truth for a moment.

Such narratives of gross injustice serve to chasten us, but they also offer us a timely reminder of the privileges we possess in our largely literate society. For every teacher, we should be humbled by the opportunity to change a life with the treasured opportunity to read widely and well. It is a timely reminder that we should tend to our classroom bookshelves alongside those of our pupils and that how well we teach reading is vital and how much emphasis we give it in our school development plans matters.

Reading and readers have always been under threat in one guise or another. Barnaby Rich, a writer and soldier, writing in 1613, stated:

> One of the diseases of this age is the multiplicity of books; they doth so overcharge the world that it is not

able to digest the abundance of idle matter that is every
day hatched and brought forth into the world.

Barnaby Rich quoted in *A History of Information
Retrieval and Storage*, by F. Stockwell, p. 172[22]

The great irony of course is that perhaps, in our present
day, it is a multitude of books, and children reading them
with skill and will, that will stave off the diseases of *our* age.

We have a long way to go. A global study by the
Organisation for Economic Development (OECD) in 2013
showed that our generation of 16- to 24-year-olds have literacy levels below that of their grandparents.[23] Consider
what that reveals about the truth about social mobility and
the looming threat posed by closing libraries and shrinking
school budgets. Perhaps this is the true disease of our age?

For pupils like Rebecca, reading well can gift her with
choices and experiences that were previously closed off to
her. There is no singular moment of freedom, nor a grand
'Hollywood ending' here. Instead, we have the slow, careful
tending to reading ability, reading access and practice.
Such reading supports no doubt matter to every pupil in
ways that far surpass the necessary, but insufficient, aim
of a set of good qualifications.

We can, and should, be passionate about reading for
both pleasure and purpose. We should be passionate about
communicating the big ideas of our subject disciplines and
the best that has been thought and said in our culture. But
being passionate about reading will not be enough.

Training every teacher to be an expert in reading
should be our aim, so that they can make the informed,
expert decisions that should define our professionalism.
Crucially then, transforming that professional knowledge
into improved teaching and learning gifts power to our
pupils in countless profound ways.

And so, we return to the six steps, distilled for clarity, to close the reading gap:

1. Train teachers to be expert in how pupils 'learn to read' and go on to 'read to learn'.
2. Develop and teach a coherent and cumulative 'reading-rich' curriculum.
3. Teach with a focus on reading access, practice and enhancing reading ability.
4. Teach, model and scaffold pupils' reading, so that they become strategic and knowledgeable readers.
5. Nurture pupils' motivation to read with purpose and for pleasure.
6. Foster a reading culture and curriculum within, and beyond, the school gates.

Hopefully, supported and emboldened by some of the ideas and insights from this book, you can pursue putting these steps into action and support every child in your care to read successfully.

Thank you for being a reader – a teacher – and a teacher who reads.

May you read forever freely.

Notes

1 Save the Children (2014). *Read on, get on: How reading can help children escape poverty.* London: Save the Children.
2 Rundell, K. (2019). Words for life interview. Retrieved from www.wordsforlife.org.uk/katherine-rundell.
3 Fielding-Barnsley, R. (2010). Australian pre-service teachers' knowledge of phonemic awareness and phonics in the process of reading. *Australian Journal of Reading Difficulties, 15*(1), 99–110; Moats, L. (2009). Still wanted: Teachers with knowledge of language. *Journal of Reading Disabilities,*

42(5), 387–391; Hurry, J., Nunes, T., Bryant, P., & Pretzlik, U. (2005). Transforming research on phonology into teacher practice. *Research Papers in Education, 20*(2): 187–206.

4 Personal communication with author, summer 2017.

5 See the handy booklet from the 'Excellence Gateway', retrieved from www.excellencegateway.org.uk/content/etf1257.

6 Adapted from Klein, C. (1993). *Diagnosing dyslexia: A guide to the assessment of adults with specific learning difficulties.* Retrieved from https://files.eric.ed.gov/fulltext/ ED356398.pdf.

7 For more on assessing vocabulary knowledge, see chapter 8 'Next steps' in Quigley, A. (2018). *Closing the vocabulary gap.* Abingdon, UK: Routledge.

8 See the excellent Reading Rockets website for more on classroom vocabulary assessment: www.readingrockets.org/article/classroom-vocabulary-assessment-content-areas.

9 Francis, D. J., Fletcher, J. M., Catts, H. W., & Tomblin, J. B. (2005). Dimensions affecting the assessment of reading comprehension. In S. G. Paris & S. A. Stahl (Eds.), *Children's reading comprehension and assessment* (pp. 369–394). Mahwah, NJ: Lawrence Erlbaum Associates.

10 Caldwell, J. (2008). *Comprehension assessment: A classroom guide.* New York, NY: Guilford Press.

11 See www.cori.umd.edu/measures/MRQ.pdf.

12 Mol, S. E., & Bus, A. G. (2011). To read or not to read: A meta-analysis of print exposure from infancy to early adolescence. *Psychological Bulletin, 137*(2), 267–296.

13 Roberts, J., Winter, K., & Connolly, P. (2017). The Letterbox Club book gifting intervention: Findings from a qualitative evaluation accompanying a randomised trial. *Children and Youth Services Review, 73,* 467–473.

14 Kraft, M. A., & Monti-Nussbaum, M. (2017). Can schools enable parents to prevent summer learning loss? A text-messaging field experiment to promote literacy skills. *Annals of the American Academy of Political and Social Science, 674*(1), 85–112.

15 Maxwell, B., Connolly, P., Demack, S., O'Hare, L., Stevens, A., Clague, L., & Stiell, B. (2014). *Summer active reading programme: Evaluation report and executive summary. Project report.* London: Education Endowment Foundation.

16 Education Endowment Foundation (2018). *Putting evidence to work: A school's guide to implementation*. London: Education Endowment Foundation.

17 Cremin, T., Mottram, M., Collins, F. M., Powell, S., & Safford, K. (2014). *Building communities of engaged readers: Reading for pleasure*. Abingdon, UK: Routledge.

18 Scarborough, H. S. (2001). Connecting early language and literacy to later reading (dis)abilities: Evidence, theory, and practice. In S. Neuman & D. Dickinson (Eds.), *Handbook for research in early literacy* (pp. 97–110). New York, NY: Guilford Press.

19 Oakhill, J. V., Cain, K., & Elbro, K. (2014). *Understanding reading comprehension: A handbook*. Abingdon, UK: Routledge; Hobsbaum, A., Gamble, N., & Reedy, D. (2010). *Guided reading at key stage 2: A handbook for teaching guided reading at key stage 2*. London: Institute of Education Publications.

20 Lemov, D. (2016). *Reading reconsidered: A practical guide to rigorous literacy instruction*. San Francisco, CA: Jossey-Bass.

21 Baker, T. L., & Baker, J. P. (1996). *The WPA Oklahoma slave narratives*. Oklahoma: University of Oklahoma Press, p. 129.

22 Stockwell, F. (2007). *A history of information storage and retrieval*. Jefferson, NC: McFarland & Co., p. 172.

23 OECD (2013). *Survey of adult skills (PIAAC). Country notes: England and Northern Ireland*. Retrieved from www.oecd.org/skills/piaac/Country%20note%20-%20United%20Kingdom.pdf.

Appendix

Name _____

Multidimensional fluency rubric[1]

	1	2	3	4
Expression and volume	Reads in a quiet voice as if to get words out The reading does not sound natural, like talking to a friend	Reads in a quiet voice The reading sounds natural in part of the text, but the reader does not always sound like they are talking to a friend	Reads with volume and expression However, sometimes the reader slips into expressionless reading and does not sound like they are talking to a friend	Reads with varied volume and expression The reader sounds like they are talking to a friend with their voice matching the interpretation of the passage
Phrasing	Reads word by word in a monotone voice	Reads in two or three word phrases, not adhering to punctuation, stress and intonation	Reads with a mixture of run-ons, mid-sentence pauses for breath and some choppiness There is reasonable stress and intonation	Reads with good phrasing, adhering to punctuation, stress and intonation

	1	2	3	4
Smoothness	Frequently hesitates while reading, sounds out words and repeats words or phrases The reader makes multiple attempts to read the same passage	Reads with extended pauses or hesitations The reader has many 'rough spots'	Reads with occasional breaks in rhythm The reader has difficulty with specific words and/ or sentence structures	Reads smoothly with some breaks, but self-corrects with difficult words and/ or sentence structures
Pace	Reads slowly and laboriously	Reads moderately slowly	Reads generally at an appropriate rate	Reads at an appropriate conversational pace

Scores of 10 or more indicate that the student is making good progress in fluency. Score _____

Note

1 Adapted from Zutell, J., & Rasinski, T. V. (1991). Training teachers to attend to their students' oral reading fluency. *Theory to Practice, 30,* 211–217.

Appendix

Vowels		Consonant	
IPA/sound	Examples	IPA/sound	Examples
/i:/ (ee)	Seat, green, tree, relief	/p/ (p)	Pull, stop, apple
/i/ (i)	Sit, grin, fish	/b/ (b)	Bet, about, beer
/ʊ/ (short oo)	Good, foot, pull	/h/ (h)	Hot, head, heart
/u:/ (long oo)	Food, rule, shoe	/f/ (f)	Four, food, fish
/e/ (e)	Head, bet, said	/v/ (v)	Observer, vow, vote
/ə/ (uh)	Teacher, observer, about	/m/ (m)	Money, lamb, my
/ɜ:/ (er)	Girl, nurse, earth	/t/ (t)	Tree, stop, want
/ɔ:/ (or)	Walk, door, four	/d/ (d)	Door, food, huddle
/a/ (a)	Had, lamb, apple	/n/ (n)	Grin, green, nurse
/ʌ/ (u)	Cup, love, money	/θ/ (th)	Earth, thigh, throw (unvoiced)
/a:/ (ar/ah)	Heart, dark, fast	/d/ (th)	They, there, bathe (voiced)
/ɒ/ (o)	Hot, stop, want	/ŋ/ (ng)	Sing, English, drank
Diphthongs		/tʃ/ (ch)	Teacher, chair, choice
/ɪə/ (eer)	Year, beer, ear	/dʒ/ (j)	Joke, joy, lounge, ridge
/eə/ (air)	Chair, where, there	/r/ (r)	Rule, grin, tree
/əʊ/ (oh)	Joke, vote, throw	/s/ (s)	Stop, since, city, pseudonym
/aʊ/ (ow)	Vow, lounge, out	/z/ (z)	Observe, noise, President
/eɪ/ (ay)	They, bathe, way	/l/ (l)	Pull, love, rule
/aɪ/ (igh)	Thigh, dice, my	/ʃ/ (sh)	Shoe, fish, sure, Pollution
/ɔɪ/ (oi)	Joy, noise, choice	/ʒ/ (zh)	Casual, measure, Pleasure
		/w/ (w)	Want, way, where
		/k/ (k)	Walk, dark, cup, plaque
		/g/ (g)	Green, grin, girl
		/j/ (y)	Year, yes, yellow

Bibliography

Adler, M. J., & Doren, C. V. (2014). *How to read a book: The classic guide to intelligent reading*. New York, NY: Simon & Schuster.

Alexander, J., & Jarman, R. (2018). The pleasures of reading non-fiction. *Literacy, 52*(2). https://doi.org/10.1111/lit.12152.

Allington, R. L. (2014). How reading volume affects both reading fluency and reading achievement. *International Electronic Journal of Elementary Education, 7*(1), 13–26.

Alloway, T. P., Williams, S., Jones, B., & Cochrane, F. (2014). Exploring the impact of television watching on vocabulary skills in toddlers. *Early Childhood Education Journal, 42*(5), 343–349.

Amzil, A. (2014). The effect of a metacognitive intervention on college students' reading performance and metacognitive skills. *Journal of Educational and Developmental Psychology, 4*(1), 27–45.

Ann Evans, M., & Saint-Aubin, J. (2005). What children are looking at during shared storybook reading: Evidence from eye movement monitoring. *Psychological Science, 16*(11), 913–920. https://doi.org/10.1111/j.1467-9280.2005.01636.x.

AQA (2016). Making questions clear: GCSE science exams from 2018. Retrieved from https://filestore.aqa.org.uk/resources/science/AQA-GCSE-SCIENCE-QUESTIONS-CLEAR.PDF.

AQA (2016), Our exams explained: GCSE science exams from Summer 2018. Retrieved from https:// filestore.aqa.org.uk/resources/science/AQA-GCSE-SCIENCE-EXAMSEXPLAINED.PDF.

Bacon, F. (n.d.). Of studies. In *Essays of Francis Bacon*. Retrieved from www.authorama.com/essays-of-francis-bacon-50.html.

Baines , L. (1996). From page to screen: When a novel is interpreted for film, what gets lost in the translation? *Journal of Adolescent & Adult Literacy, 39*(8), 612–622.

Bibliography

Baker, T. L., & Baker, J. P. (1996). *The WPA Oklahoma slave narratives.* Oklahoma: University of Oklahoma Press.

Barton, S. B., & Sanford, A. J. (1993). A case study of anomaly detection: Shallow semantic processing and cohesion establishment. *Memory and Cognition, 21*(4), 477–487.

BBC News (2019). Mr Greedy 'almost as hard to read' as Steinbeck Classics. Retrieved from www.bbc.co.uk/news/uk-47426551.

Beck, I., & McKeown, M. G. (2002). Questioning the author: Making sense of social studies. *Reading and Writing in the Content Areas, 60*(3), 44–47.

Beck, I., McKeown, M., & Kucan, L. (2002). *Bringing words to life.* New York, NY: Guilford Press.

Beck, I., & Sandora, C. (2016). *Illuminating comprehension and close reading.* New York, NY: Guilford Press.

Bergman, J. (2012). *Hitler and the Nazi Darwinian worldview: How the Nazi eugenic crusade for a superior race caused the greatest Holocaust in world history.* Ontario, Canada: Joshua Press.

Best, R. M., Floyd, R. G., & Mcnamara, D. S. (2008). Differential competencies contributing to children's comprehension of narrative and expository texts. *Reading Psychology, 29*(2), 137–164. doi:10.1080/02702710801963951.

Biber, D., & Gray, B. (2016). *Grammatical complexity in academic English.* Cambridge, UK: Cambridge University Press.

Biemiller, A. (2000). Teaching vocabulary. *American Educator,* Spring, 24–28.

Blythe, H., & Joseph, H. S. S. (2011). Children's eye movements during reading. In S. P. Liversedge, I. Gilchrist, & S. Everling (Eds.), *The Oxford handbook of eye movements* (pp. 643–662). Oxford: Oxford University Press.

Booker, C. (2004). *Seven basic plots: Why we tell stories.* New York, NY: Continuum Books.

Breadmore, H., Vardy , E. J., Cunningham , A. J., Kwok, R. K. W., & Carroll, J. M. (2019). *Literacy development: A review of the evidence.* Retrieved from https://educationendowmentfoundation.org.uk/public/files/Literacy_Development_Evidence_Review.pdf.

Bromley, K. (2007). Nine things every teacher should know about words and vocabulary instruction. *Journal of Adolescent & Adult Literacy, 50*(7), 528–537.

Brown, L. T., Mohr, K. A. J., Wilcox, B. R., & Barrett, T. S. (2018). The effects of dyad reading and text difficulty on third-graders' reading achievement. *Journal of Educational Research, 111*(5), 541–553. doi:10.1080/00220671.2017.1310711.

Bryce, N. (2011). Meeting the reading challenges of science textbooks in the primary grades. *The Reading Teacher, 64*(7), 474–485.

Brysbaert, M. (2019). *How many words do we read per minute? A review and meta-analysis of reading rate.* https://doi.org/10.31234/osf.io/xynwg. PsyArXiv preprint.

Burns, M. K., Appleton, J. J., & Stehouwer, J. D. (2005). Meta-analytic review of responsiveness-to-intervention research: Examining field-based and research-implemented models. *Journal of Psychoeducational Assessment, 23*, 381–394.

Butler, S., Urrutia, K., Buenger, A., Gonzalez, N., Hunt, M., & Eisenhart, C. (2010). *A review of the current research on vocabulary instruction.* Portsmouth, NH: National Reading Technical Assistance Center.

Cain, K., & Oakhill, J. V. (1998). Comprehension skills and inference-making ability: Issues of causality. In C. Hulme & R. M. Joshi (Eds.), *Reading and spelling: Development and disorders* (pp. 329–342). Princeton, NJ: Lawrence Erlbaum Associates.

Cain, K., & Oakhill, J. V. (1999). Inference making and its relation to comprehension failure. *Reading and Writing, 11*, 489–503.

Cain, K., & Oakhill, J. V. (2006). Profiles of children with specific reading comprehension difficulties. *British Journal of Educational Psychology, 76*(4), 683–696. https://doi.org/10.1348/000709905X67610.

Cain, K., & Oakhill, J. V. (2007). Reading comprehension difficulties: Correlates, causes and consequences. In K. Cain & J. V. Oakhill (Eds.), *Children's comprehension problems in oral and written language* (pp. 41–76). New York, NY: Guilford Press.

Cain, K., Oakhill, J. V., Barnes, M. A., & Bryant, P. E. (2001). Comprehension skill, inference-making ability, and their relation to knowledge. *Memory & Cognition, 29*, 850–859.

Cain, K., Oakhill, J. V., & Elbro, C. (2003). The ability to learn new word meanings from context by school-age children with and without language comprehension difficulties. *Journal of Child Language, 30*, 681–694.

Cain, K., & Towse, A. S. (2008). To get hold of the wrong end of the stick: Reasons for poor idiom understanding in children with reading comprehension difficulties. *Journal of Speech, Language, and Hearing Research, 51*(6), 1538–1549. https://doi.org/10.1044/1092-4388(2008/07-0269.

Cain, S. (2018). Nearly 130 public libraries closed across Britain in the last year. *Guardian.* Retrieved from www.theguardian.com/books/2018/dec/07/nearly-130-public-libraries-closed-across-britain-in-the-last-year.

Bibliography

Caldwell, J. (2008). *Comprehension assessment: A classroom guide.* New York, NY: Guilford Press.

Camden, B. (2017). Single textbook approved for maths mastery teaching. *Schools Week,* 21 July. Retrieved from https://schoolsweek.co.uk/single-textbook-approved-for-maths-mastery-teaching.

Cameron, S. (2009). *Teaching reading comprehension strategies.* New Zealand: Pearson.

Carrier, S. J. (2011). *Effective strategies for teaching science vocabulary.* UNC-Chapel Hill, NC, LEARN North Carolina. Retrieved from www.learnnc.org/lp/pages/7079.

Carver, R. (1992). Reading rate: Theory, research, and practical implications. *Journal of Reading, 36*(2), 84–95. Retrieved from www.jstor.org/stable/40016440.

Castles, A., Rastle, K., & Nation, K. (2018). Ending the reading wars: Reading acquisition from novice to expert. *Psychological Science in the Public Interest, 19,* 5–51. doi:10.1177/1529100618772271.

Centre for Literacy in Primary Education (2019). *Reflecting realities: A survey of ethnic representation within UK children's literature 2018.* Retrieved from https://clpe.org.uk/publications-and-bookpacks/reflecting-realities/reflecting-realities-survey-ethnic-representation.

Cesi, S. J., & Papierno, P. B. (2005). The rhetoric and reality of gap closing: When the 'have nots' gain but the 'haves' gain even more. *American Psychologist, 60*(2), 149–160.

Chall, J. S., Jacobs, V. A., & Baldwin, L. E. (1990). *The reading crisis: Why poor children fall behind.* Cambridge, MA: Harvard University Press.

Chambers, A. (1993). *Tell me: Children, reading and talk.* Stroud, UK: Thimble Press.

Chapman, J., Tunmer, W., & Prochnow, J. (2000). Early reading-related skills and performance, reading self-concept, and the development of academic self-concept: A longitudinal study. *Journal of Educational Psychology, 92,* 703–708. doi:10.1037/0022-0663.92.4.703.

Chard, D. J., Vaughn, S., & Tyler, B. -J. (2002). A synthesis of research on effective interventions for building reading fluency with elementary students with learning disabilities. *Journal of Learning Disabilities, 35*(5), 386–406.

Chen, X., & Meurers, D. (2018). Word frequency and readability: Predicting the text-level readability with a lexical-level attribute. *Journal of Research in Reading, 41*(3), 486–510.

Ciardiello, A. V., & Cicchelli, T. (1994). The effects of instructional training models and content knowledge on student questioning in social studies. *Journal of Social Studies Research, 19,* 30–37.

Clark, C., & Picton , I. (2018). *Book ownership, literacy engagement and mental wellbeing.* London: National Literacy Trust.

Clarke, P. J., Snowling, M. J., Truelove, E., & Hulme, C. (2010). Ameliorating children's reading comprehension difficulties: A randomised controlled trial. *Psychological Science, 21*, 1106–1116. doi:10.1177/0956797610375449.

Clarke, P. J., Truelove, E., Hulme, C., & Snowling, M. J. (2013). *Developing reading comprehension.* Chichester, UK: John Wiley & Sons.

Clarke, R. (2018). *The 2018 KS2 reading SATs: Expert analysis.* Retrieved from https://freedomtoteach.collins.co.uk/the-2018-ks2-reading-sats-expert-analysis.

Clemens, N. H., Ragan, K., & Widales-Benitez, O. (2016). Reading difficulties in young children: Beyond basic early literacy skills. *Policy Insights from the Behavioral and Brain Sciences, 3*(2), 177–184.

Conti, G. (2016). *Eleven low-preparation/high-impact tips for enhancing reading tasks.* Retrieved from https://bit.ly/2KUPjft.

Counsell, C. (2004). *History in practice: History and literacy in Y7 – building the lesson around the text.* London: Hodder Murray.

Counsell, C., Fordham, M., Foster, R., & Burn, K. (2016). *Teaching History: Scales of Planning Edition, 162,* March.

Counsell, C., Fordham, M., Foster, R., & Burn, K. (2016). *Teaching History: Excited and Carry On Edition, 163,* June.

Counsell, C. (2018). *Senior curriculum leadership 1: The indirect manifestation of knowledge: (A) curriculum as narrative.* Retrieved from https://thedignityofthethingblog.wordpress.com.

Coxhead, A. (2000). A new academic word list. *TESOL Quarterly, 34*(2), 213–238.

Crawford, H. (2017). *Oxford international primary history: Workbook 2.* Oxford: Oxford University Press.

Cremin, T., Mottram, M., Bearne, E., & Goodwin, P. (2008). Exploring teachers' knowledge of children's literature. *Cambridge Journal of Education, 38*(4), 449–464.

Cremin, T., Mottram, M., Bearne, E., & Goodwin, P. (2008). Primary teachers as readers. *English in Education, 41*(1), 8–23.

Cremin, T., Mottram, M., Collins, F. M., Powell, S., & Safford, K. (2014). *Building communities of engaged readers: Reading for pleasure.* Abingdon, UK: Routledge.

Crystal, D. (2007). *Words, words, words.* New York, NY: Oxford University Press.

Cunningham, A. E., & Stanovich, K. E. (1998). What reading does for the mind. *American Educator, 22*, 8–15.

Dahl, R. (2001). *The witches.* London: Puffin Books.

Davis, M. H., McPartland, J. M., Pryseski, C., & Kim, E. (2018). The effects of coaching on English teachers' reading instruction practices and adolescent students' reading comprehension. *Literacy Research and Instruction, 57*(3), 255–275. doi:10.1080/19388071.2018.1453897.

Bibliography

Dawson, N., Rastle, K., & Ricketts, J. (2018). Morphological effects in visual word recognition: Children, adolescents, and adults. *Journal of Experimental Psychology: Learning, memory and cognition, 44*(4), 645–654.

de Glopper, K., & Swanborn, M. S. L. (1999). Incidental word learning while reading: A meta-analysis. *Review of Educational Research, 69*(3), 261–285. https://doi.org/(...)02/00346543069003261.

Delgado, P., Vargas, C., Ackerman, R., & Salmeron, L. (2018). Don't throw away your printed books: A meta-analysis on the effects of reading media on reading comprehension. *Educational Research Review, 25*, 23–38.

Department for Education (2013). *Science programmes of study: Key stages 1 and 2 – national curriculum in England.* London: Department for Education.

Department for Education (2018). *The childcare and early years survey of parents 2017.* Retrieved from https://assets.publishing. service.gov.uk/government/uploads/system/uploads/attachment_ data/file/766498/Childcare_and_Early_Years_Survey_of_Parents_in_ England_2018.pdf.

Department for Education (2018). *2018 key stage 1 teacher assessment exemplification: English reading – working at the expected standard.* Retrieved from https://assets.publishing.service.gov.uk/ government/uploads/system/uploads/attachment_data/file/762975/ 2018_key_stage_1_teacher_assessment_exemplification_expected_ standard.pdf.

Department for Education (2018). *2018 national curriculum assessments: Key stage 1 phonics screening check, national assessments.* Retrieved from https://assets.publishing.service.gov. uk/government/uploads/system/uploads/attachment_data/file/ 715823/2018_phonics_pupils_materials_standard.pdf.pdf.

Department for Education (2019). *2019 key stage 2 English reading test mark schemes Reading answer booklet.* Retrieved from https:// assets.publishing.service.gov.uk/government/uploads/system/ uploads/attachment_data/file/803889/STA198212e_2019_ks2_ English_reading_Mark_schemes.pdf.

Department for Education (2019). *National curriculum assessments at key stage 2 in England, 2019 (interim).* Retrieved from www.gov. uk/government/publications/national-curriculum-assessments-key-stage-2-2019-interim/national-curriculum-assessments-at-key-stage-2-in-england-2019-interim.

Department for Education: Education Standards Research Team (2012). *Research evidence on reading for pleasure.* London: Department for Education.

Dickinson, D. K., Griffith, J. A., Golinkoff, R. M., & Hirsh-Pasek, K. (2012). How reading books fosters language development around the world. *Child Development Research.* http://dx.doi.org/10.1155/2012/602807.

Dictionary.com (2018). Which words did English take from other languages? Retrieved from www.dictionary.com/e/borrowed-words.

Dougherty Stahl, K. A., & Bravo, M. A. (2010). Contemporary classroom vocabulary assessment for content areas. *The Reading Teacher, 63*(7), 566–578.

Dunlosky, J., & Rawson, K. A. (2012). Overconfidence produces under-achievement: Inaccurate self-evaluations undermine students' learning and retention. *Learning and Instruction, 22,* 271–280. Retrieved from https://pdfs.semanticscholar.org/b0bb/624eb91d713 137f7a8a2a93952cf72750f29.pdf.

Eagleton, T. (2014). *How to read literature.* New Haven, CT: Yale University Press.

Education Endowment Foundation (2017). *Improving literacy in key stage 1.* London: Education Endowment Foundation.

Education Endowment Foundation (2017). *Improving literacy in key stage 2.* London: Education Endowment Foundation.

Education Endowment Foundation (2017). *Making best use of teaching assistants.* London: Education Endowment Foundation.

Education Endowment Foundation (2018). *Making best use of teaching assistants.* London: Education Endowment Foundation.

Education Endowment Foundation (2018). *Metacognition and self-regulation.* London: Education Endowment Foundation.

Education Endowment Foundation (2018). *Preparing for literacy: Improving communication, language and literacy in the early years.* London: Education Endowment Foundation.

Education Endowment Foundation (2018). *Putting evidence to work: A school's guide to implementation.* London: Education Endowment Foundation.

Education Endowment Foundation (2019). *Improving literacy in secondary schools.* London: Education Endowment Foundation.

Education Endowment Foundation (2019). *Peer tutoring: Toolkit strand.* Retrieved from https://educationendowmentfoundation.org.uk/evidence-summaries/teaching-learning-toolkit/peer-tutoring.

Education Endowment Foundation (2019). *Reciprocal reading.* Retrieved from https://educationendowmentfoundation.org.uk/pdf/generate/?u=https://educationendowmentfoundation.org.uk/pdf/project/?id=956&t=EEF%20Projects&e=956&s=.

Education Endowment Foundation (2019). *Working with parents to support children's learning.* London: Education Endowment Foundation.

Bibliography

Ehri, L. C., & McCormick, S. (1998). Phrases of word learning: Implications for instruction with delayed and disabled readers. *Reading & Writing Quarterly, 14*(2), 135–163. doi:10.1080/1057356980140202.

Elleman, A. (2017). Examining the impact of inference instruction on the literal and inferential comprehension of skilled and less skilled readers: A meta-analytic review. *Journal of Educational Psychology, 109*. doi:10.1037/edu0000180.

Elliott, J. G., & Grigorenko, E. L. (2014). *The dyslexia debate.* New York, NY: Cambridge University Press.

Ellman, A. M., Lindo, E. J., Morphy, P., & Compton, D. L. (2009). The impact of vocabulary instruction on passage-level comprehension of school-age children: A meta-analysis. *Journal of Research on Educational Effectiveness, 2*(1), 1–44.

Ellroy, J. (2010). *American tabloid.* London: Windmill Books.

Eunice Kennedy Shriver National Institute of Child Health and Human Development, NIH, DHHS (2010). *What content-area teachers should know about adolescent literacy (NA).* Washington, DC: US Government Printing Office.

Evans, M. D. R., Kelly, K., Sikora, J., & Treiman, D. J. (2010). Family scholarly culture and educational success: Books and schooling in 27 nations. *Research in Social Stratification and Mobility, 28*(2), 171–197.

Fang, Z., & Schleppegrell, M. J. (2010). Disciplinary literacies across content areas: Supporting secondary reading through functional language analysis. *Journal of Adolescent & Adult Literacy, 53*(7), 587–597. doi:10.1598/JAAL.53.7.6.

Ferreiro, E., & Teberosky, A. (1982). *Literacy before schooling.* Portsmouth, NH: Heinemann Educational Books.

Fielding-Barnsley, R. (2010). Australian pre-service teachers' knowledge of phonemic awareness and phonics in the process of reading. *Australian Journal of Reading Difficulties, 15*(1), 99–110.

Finkel, I., & Taylor, J. (2015). *Cuneifrom.* London: British Museum Press.

Fleming, M., Smith, P., & Worden, D. (2016). *GCSE religious studies for AQA A: GCSE Islam.* Oxford: Oxford University Press.

Foster, R. (2013). The more things change, the more they stay the same: Developing students' thinking about change and continuity. *Teaching History, 151,* 8–17.

Francis, D. J., Fletcher, J. M., Catts, H. W., & Tomblin, J. B. (2005). Dimensions affecting the assessment of reading comprehension. In S. G. Paris & S. A. Stahl (Eds.), *Children's reading comprehension and assessment* (pp. 369–394). Mahwah, NJ: Lawrence Erlbaum Associates.

Fricke, S., Bowyer-Crane, C., Haley, A. J., Hulme, C., & Snowling, M. J. (2013). Efficacy of language intervention in the early years. *Journal of Child Psychology and Psychiatry, 54*(3), 280–290.

Fuentes, P. (1998). Reading comprehension in mathematics. *The Clearing House, 72*(2), 81–88. doi:10.1080/00098659809599602.

Fulmer, S. M., & Frijters, J. C. (2011). Motivation during an excessively challenging reading task: The buffering role of relative topic interest. *Journal of Experimental Education, 79*(2), 185–208.

Gamble, N. (2013). *Exploring children's literature: Reading with pleasure and purpose.* London: Sage.

Gambrell, L. B. (2011). Seven rules of engagement: What's most important to know about motivation to read. *The Reading Teacher, 65*(3), 172–178.

Gambrell, L. B. (2015). Getting students hooked on the reading habit. *The Reading Teacher, 69*(3), 259–263.

Gardner, T. (2003). Drop everything, and read! Retrieved from https://eric.ed.gov/?id=ED476414.

Gelzheiser, L. M., Scanlon, D. M., Hallgren-Flynn, L., & Connors, P. (2019). *Comprehensive reading intervention in grades 3–8: Fostering word learning, comprehension, and motivation.* London: Guilford Press.

The Geographical Association (n.d.). Coasts lesson plans: Look at it this way lesson 8. Retrieved from www.geography.org.uk/download/ga_hydrologycoastsl8informationsheet8.pdf.

Gilkerson, J., Richards, J. A., & Topping, K. (2017). The impact of book reading in the early years on parent–child language interaction. *Journal of Early Childhood Literacy, 17*(1), 92–110. doi:10.1177/1468798415608907.

Gladfelter, I., Barron, K. L., & Johnson, E. (2019). Visual and verbal semantic productions in children with ASD, DLD, and typical language. *Journal of Communication Disorders, 82*, 105921. https://doi.org/10.1016/j.jcomdis.2019.105921.

Gladwell, M. (2014). *David and Goliath: Underdogs, misfits and the art of battling giants.* London: Penguin.

Glenberg, A. M., Meyer, M., & Lindem, K. (1987). Mental models contribute to foregrounding during text comprehension. *Journal of Memory and Language, 26*(1), 69–83.

Goldman, S. R., Britt, M. A., Brown, W., Cribb, G., George, M., Greenleaf, C. ... Project READI. (2016). Disciplinary literacies and learning to read for understanding: A conceptual framework for disciplinary literacy. *Educational Psychologist, 51*(2), 219–246. doi:10.1080/00461520.2016.1168741.

Goodwin, B. (2011). Research says ... don't wait until 4th grade to address the slump. *Educational Leadership, 68*(7). Retrieved from www.ascd.org/publications/educational-leadership/apr11/vol68/num07/Don%27t-Wait-Until-4th-Grade-to-Address-the-Slump.aspx.

Bibliography

Gough, P. B., Hoover, W. A., & Peterson, C. L. (1996). Some observations on a simple view of reading. In C. Cornoldi & J. V. Oakhill (Eds.), *Reading comprehension difficulties: Processes and interventions* (pp. 1–13). Mahwah, NJ: Lawrence Erlbaum Associates.

Gough, P. B., & Tunmer, W. E. (1986). Decoding, reading, and reading disability. *Remedial and Special Education, 7*, 6–10.

Graham, S. (1999). Handwriting and spelling instruction for students with learning disabilities: A review. *Learning Disability Quarterly, 22*(2), 78–98.

Graham, S., & Hebert, M. A. (2010). *Writing to read: Evidence for how writing can improve reading. A Carnegie Corporation time to act report.* Washington, DC: Alliance for Excellent Education.

Graham, S., & Hebert, M. (2011). Writing to read: A meta-analysis of the impact of writing and writing instruction on reading. *Harvard Educational Review, 81*(4), 710–744. doi:10.17763/haer.81.4.t2kom 13756113566.

Graham, S., Liu, X., Aitken, A., Ng, C., Bartlett, B., Harris, K., & Holzapfel, J. (2017). Effectiveness of literacy programs balancing reading and writing instruction: A meta-analysis. *Reading Research Quarterly, 53*(3), 279–304. doi:10.1002/rrq.194.

Great School Libraries (2019). *Great school libraries survey findings and update on phase 1.* London: Great School Libraries.

Greene, G. (1999). The lost childhood. In G. Greene, *Collected essays.* London: Vintage.

Grenby, M. O. (2014). *The origins of children's literature.* Retrieved from www.bl.uk/romantics-and-victorians/articles/the-origins-of-childrens-literature?_ga=2.199556525.2090890301.154992653 2-624299337.1549926532.

Griffiths, Y. M., & Snowling, M. J. (2002). Predictors of exception word and nonword reading in dyslexic children: The severity hypothesis. *Journal of Educational Psychology, 94*(1), 34–43. http://dx.doi.org/10.1037/0022-0663.94.1.34.

Hamilton, L. G., Hayiou-Thomas, M. E., Hulme, C., & Snowling, M. J. (2016). The home literacy environment as a predictor of the early literacy development of children at family-risk of dyslexia. *Scientific Studies of Reading, 20*(5), 401–419. doi:10.1080/10888438.2016.1213266.

Hart, B., & Risley, T. R. (1995). *Meaningful differences in the everyday experiences of young American children: The everyday experience of one- and two-year-old American children.* Baltimore, MD: Paul H. Brookes.

Hasbrouck, J., & Tindal, G. (2017). *An update to compiled ORF norms (technical report no. 1702).* Eugene, OR: Behavioral Research and Teaching, University of Oregon.

Hatcher, P. J., Hulme, C., Miles, J. N. V., Carroll, J. M., Hatcher, J., Smith, G., & Gibbs, S. (2006). Efficacy of small-group reading intervention for beginning readers with reading delay: A randomised controlled trial. *Journal of Child Psychology & Psychiatry, 47*(8), 820–827. https://doi.org/10.1111/j.1469-7610.2005.01559.x.

Henderson, L. M., Tsogka, N., & Snowling, M. J. (2013). Questioning the benefits that coloured overlays can have for reading in students with and without dyslexia. *Jorsen, 13*, 57–65.

Herman, P., & Wardrip, P. (2012). Reading to learn: Helping students comprehend reading in science class. *The Science Teacher, 79*(1), 48–51.

Hillman, A. M. (2014). A literature review on disciplinary literacy: How do secondary teachers apprentice students into mathematical literacy? *Journal of Adolescent & Adult Literacy, 57*(5), 397–406. doi:10.1002/jaal.256.

Hirsch, E. D. (1994). *Cultural literacy: What every American needs to know.* Boulder, CO: Westview Press.

Hirsch, E. D. (2003). Reading comprehension requires knowledge – of words and the world. *American Educator, 27*(1), 10–13.

Hirsch, E. D., Jr (2000). You can always look it up – or can you. *American Educator, 24*(1), 4–9.

Hirsch, E. D., Jr (2013). A wealth of words. The key to increasing upward mobility is expanding vocabulary. *City Journal, 23*(1). Retrieved from www.cityjournal.org/html/wealth-words- 13523.html.

Hirsch, E. D., Jr, & Moats, L. C. (2001). Overcoming the language gap. *American Educator, 25*(2), 4–9.

Hobsbaum, A., Gamble, N., & Reedy, D. (2010). *Guided reading at key stage 2: A handbook for teaching guided reading at key stage 2.* London: Institute of Education Publications.

Hurry, J., Nunes, T., Bryant, P., & Pretzlik, U. (2005). Transforming research on phonology into teacher practice. *Research Papers in Education, 20*(2), 187–206.

International Literacy Association (2018). *Reading fluently does not mean reading fast.* Newark, DE: Author.

Jenner, T. (2019). Making reading routine: Helping KS3 pupils to become regular readers of historical scholarship. *Teaching History,* March, 42–48.

Jerrim, J. (2013). *The reading gap: The socio-economic gap in children's reading skills: A cross-national comparison using PISA 2009.* London: Sutton Trust.

Jerrim, J., & Moss, G. (2019). The link between fiction and teenagers: Reading skills: International evidence from the OECD PISA study. *British Educational Research Journal, 45*(1), 181–200.

Johnson, H., Watson, P. A., Delahunty, T., McSwiggen, P., & Smith, T. (2011). What is it they do: Differentiating knowledge and literacy practices across content disciplines. *Journal of Adolescent and Adult Literacy*, *55*(2), 100–109.

Joseph, H. S. S. L., Liversedge, S., & Nation, K. (2013). Using eye movements to investigate word frequency effects in children's sentence reading. *School Psychology Review*, *42*(2), 207–222.

Joseph, L. M., Alber-Morgan, S., Cullen, J., & Rouse, C. (2016). The effects of self-questioning on reading comprehension: A literature review. *Reading & Writing Quarterly*, *32*(2), 152–173. doi:10.1080/10573569.2014.891449.

Kaefer, T. (2018). The role of topic-related background knowledge in visual attention to illustration and children's word learning during shared book reading. *Journal of Research in Reading*, *41*(3), 582–596.

Kame'enui, E. J., & Baumann, J. F. (Eds.). (2012). *Vocabulary instruction: Research to practice*. New York, NY: Guilford Press.

Kispal, A. (2008). *Effective teaching of inference skills for reading: Literature review*. Department for Education Research Report. Retrieved from www.nfer.ac.uk/publications/EDR01/EDR01.pdf.

Klein, C. (1993). *Diagnosing dyslexia. A guide to the assessment of adults with specific learning difficulties*. Retrieved from https://files.eric.ed.gov/fulltext/ED356398.pdf.

Kolb, C. (2014). *Relationships between discourse, reader identity, and reading self-efficacy in a high school English classroom: A mixed methods, critical ethnographic study*. Minneapolis: University of Minnesota Press.

Kraft, M. A., & Monti-Nussbaum, M. (2017). Can schools enable parents to prevent summer learning loss? A text-messaging field experiment to promote literacy skills. *Annals of the American Academy of Political and Social Science*, *674*(1), 85–112.

Lapp, D., Grant, M., Moss, B., & Johnson, K. (2013). Students' close reading of science texts: What's now? What's next? *The Reading Teacher*, *67*(2), 109–119.

Laufer, B. (2017). From word parts to full texts: Searching for effective methods of vocabulary learning. *Language Teaching Research*, *21*(1), 5–11. https://doi.org/10.1177/1362168816683118.

Law, J., Charlton, J., Dockrell, J., Gascoigne, M., McKean, C., & Theakston, A. (2017). *Early language development: Needs, provision, and intervention for pre-school children from soci-economically disadvantaged backgrounds*. Newcastle University review for the Education Endowment Foundation. London: Education Endowment Foundation.

Law, J., Charlton, J., McKean, C., Beyer, F., Fernandez-Garcia, C., Mashayekhi, A., & Rush, R. (2018). *Parent–child reading to improve language development and school readiness: A systematic review and meta-analysis (final report)*. Newcastle and Edinburgh: Newcastle University & Queen Margaret University.

Lemov, D. (2016). *Reading reconsidered: A practical guide to rigorous literacy instruction.* San Francisco, CA: Jossey-Bass.

Lindgren, W., Roberts, G., & Sankey, A. (1999). *Introduction to mathematical thinking.* Retrieved from www.tec.iup.edu/mhogue/literary_review.html.

Lockiewicz, M., Bogdanowicz, K., & Bogdanowicz, M. (2013). Psychological resources of adults with developmental dyslexia. *Journal of learning disabilities, 47*(6), 543–555. doi:10.1177/0022219413478663.

Logan, J. A. R., Justice, L. M., Yumuş, M., & Chaparro-Moreno, L, J. (2019). When children are not read to at home: The million-word gap. *Journal of Developmental & Behavioral Pediatrics, 40*(5), 383–386. doi:10.1097/DBP.0000000000000657.

McCormick, S., & Zutell, J. (2015). *Instructing students who have literacy problems* (7th ed.). Boston, MA: Allyn & Bacon.

Manguel, A. (1997). *A history of reading.* London: Flamingo.

Marshall, C. M., & Nation, K. (2003). Individual differences in semantic and structural errors in children's memory for sentences. *Educational and Child Psychology, 20*(3), 7–18.

Maxwell, B., Connolly, P., Demack, S., O'Hare, L., Stevens, A., Clague, L., & Stiell, B. (2014). *Summer active reading programme: Evaluation report and executive summary. Project report.* London: Education Endowment Foundation.

Mayhew, H. (2018). *London labour and the London poor* (Vol. 3 of 4). A Project Gutenberg e-book. Retrieved from www.gutenberg.org/files/57060/57060-h/57060-h.htm#Page_43.

Melekoglu, M. A., & Wilkerson, K. L. (2013). Motivation to read: How does it change for struggling readers with and without disabilities? *International Journal of Instruction, 6*(1), 77–88.

Merrell, C., & Tymms, P. (2007). Identifying reading problems with computer-adaptive assessments. *Journal of Computer Assisted Learning, 23,* 27–35. doi:10.1111/j.1365-2729.2007.00196.x.

Meschyan, G., & Hernandez, A. (2002). Is native-language decoding skill related to second-language learning? *Journal of Educational Psychology, 94*(1), 14–22.

Meyer, J. B. F. (1985). Prose analysis: Purposes, procedures, and problems. In B. K. Britten & J. B. Black (Eds.), *Understanding expository text: A theoretical and practical handbook for analyzing explanatory text* (pp. 11–64). Hillsdale, NJ: Lawrence Erlbaum Associates.

Meyer, J. B. F. (2003). Text coherence and readability. *Topics in Language Disorders, 23*(3), 204–224. doi:10.1097/00011363-200307000-00007.

Moats, L. C. (2005). How spelling supports reading. *American Educator, 6*(12–22), 42–43.

Moats, L. (2009). Still wanted: Teachers with knowledge of language. *Journal of Reading Disabilities, 42*(5), 387–391.

Bibliography

Moje, E. B. (2008). Foregrounding the disciplines in secondary literacy teaching and learning: A call for change. *Journal of Adolescent and Adult Literacy, 52*(2), 96–107. doi:10.1598/JAAL.52.2.1.

Mol, S. E., & Bus, A. G. (2011). To read or not to read: A meta-analysis of print exposure from infancy to early adulthood. *Psychological Bulletin, 137*(2), 267–296.

Mol, S. E., Bus, A. G., de Jong, M. T., & Smeets, D. J. H. (2008). Added value of dialogic parent–child book readings: A meta-analysis. *Early Education and Development, 19*(1), 7–26. doi:10.1080/10409280701838603.

Morgan, W. P. (1896). A case of congenital word blindness. *British Medical Journal, 2*(1871), 1378. doi:10.1136/bmj.2.1871.1378.

Mullis, I. V. S., Martin, M. O., Foy, P., & Hooper, M. (2017). *PIRLS 2016 international results in reading.* Retrieved from http://timssandpirls.bc.edu/pirls2016/international-results.

Munzer, T. G., Miller, A. L., Weeks, H. M., Kaciroti, N., & Radesky, J. (2019). Differences in parent–toddler interactions with electronic versus print books. *Pediatrics, 143*(4), e20182012. doi:10.1542/peds.2018-2012.

Nagy, W., & Townsend, D. (2012). Words as tools: Learning academic vocabulary as language acquisition. *Reading Research Quarterly, 47*(1), 91–108.

Nation, K. (2017). Nurturing a lexical legacy: Reading experience is critical for the development of word reading skill. *NPJ Science of Learning, 2*(1), 3.

Nation, K., Clarke, P., & Snowling, M. J. (2002). General cognitive ability in children with reading comprehension difficulties. *British Journal of Educational Psychology, 72*(4), 549–560. http://dx.doi.org/10.1348/00070990260377604.

Nation, K., Cocksey, J., Taylor, J. S., & Bishop, D. V. (2010). A longitudinal investigation of early reading and language skills in children with poor reading comprehension. *Journal of Child Psychiatry, 51*, 1031–1039.

National Institute of Child Health and Human Development (2000). *Report of the National Reading Panel: Teaching children to read – an evidence-based assessment of the scientific research literature on reading and its implications for reading instruction* (NIH Publication No. 00-4769). Washington, DC: U.S. Government Printing Office.

National Institute for Literacy (2007). *What content-area teachers should know about adolescent literacy.* Washington, DC: National Institute for Literacy.

Nutthall, G. (2007). *The hidden lives of learners.* Wellington, NZ: NZCER Press.

Oakhill, J. V., Cain, K., & Elbro, K. (2014). *Understanding reading comprehension: A handbook*. Abingdon, UK: Routledge.

O'Brien, D. G., Moje, E. B., & Stewart, R. A. (2001). Exploring the context of secondary literacy: Literacy in people's everyday school lives. In E. B. Moje & D. G. O'Brien (Eds.), *Constructions of literacy: Studies of teaching and learning in and out of secondary classrooms* (pp. 27–48). Mahwah, NJ: Lawrence Erlbaum Associates.

Ofsted (2018). *An investigation into how to assess the quality of education through curriculum intent, implementation and impact*. No. 180035. Retrieved from https://assets.publishing.service.gov.uk/government/uploads/system/uploads/attachment_data/file/766252/How_to_assess_intent_and_implementation_of_curriculum_191218.pdf?_ga=2.94315933.1884489255.1566838991-1949876102.1566494836.

Olson, L. A., Evans, J. R., & Keckler, W. T. (2006). Precocious readers: Past, present, and future. *Journal for the Education of the Gifted, 30*(2), 205–235. https://doi.org/10.4219/jeg-2006–260.

Olson, R. K., Keenan, J. M., Byrne, B., Samuelsson, S., Coventry, W. L., Corley, R., … Hulslander, J. (2007). Genetic and environmental influences on vocabulary and reading development. *Scientific Studies of Reading: The Official Journal of the Society for the Scientific Study of Reading, 20*(1–2), 51–75. http://doi.org/10.1007/s11145-006-9018-x.

Organisation for Economic Development (OECD) (2013). *Survey of adult skills (PIAAC). Country notes: England and Northern Ireland*. Retrieved from www.oecd.org/skills/piaac/Country%20note%20-%20United%20Kingdom.pdf.

Orwell, G. (1949). *1984*. London: Penguin.

Oxford Reference (2017). *The tale of Madame d'Aulnoy*. Retrieved from https://blog.oup.com/2017/06/fairy-tale-of-madame-daulnoy.

Palincsar, A., & Brown, A. L. (1984). Reciprocal teaching of comprehension-fostering and monitoring activities. *Cognition and Instruction, 1*(2), 117–175.

Panchyshyn, R., & Monroe, E. E. (1992). Vocabulary considerations in mathematics instruction. Paper presented at the Fourteenth World Congress on Reading, Maui, HI.

Paracchini, S., Scerri, T., & Monaco, A. P. (2007). The genetic lexicon of dyslexia. *Annual Review of Genomics Human Genetics, 8*, 57–79.

Pearson, P. D., & Hamm, D. N. (2005). The assessment of reading comprehension: A review of practices-past, present, and future. In S. G. Paris & S. A. Stahl (Eds.), *Children's reading comprehension and assessment* (pp. 13–69). Mahwah, NJ: Lawrence Erlbaum Associates.

Pennac, D. (2006). *The rights of the reader*. London: Walker Books.

Bibliography

Perez, A. Joseph, H., Bajo, T., & Nation, K. (2016). Evaluation and revision of inferential comprehension in narrative texts: An eye movement study. *Language, Cognition and Neuroscience, 31*(4), 549–566.

Pichert, J. W., & Anderson, R. C. (1977). Taking different perspectives on a story. *Journal of Educational Psychology, 69*(4), 309–315. http://dx.doi.org/10.1037/0022-0663.69.4.309.

Pieper, K. (2016). *Reading for pleasure: A passport to everywhere.* Carmarthen: Crown House Publishing.

Pinker, S., & McGuiness, D. (1998). *Why children can't read and what we can do about it.* London: Penguin.

Pressley, M., Wood, E., Woloshyn, V. E., Martin, V., King, A., & Menke, D. (1992). Encouraging mindful use of prior knowledge: Attempting to construct explanatory answers facilitates learning. *Educational Psychologist, 21*(1), 91–109.

Protherough, R. (1983). *Developing a response to fiction.* Milton Keynes, UK: Open University.

Quigley, A. (2018). *Closing the vocabulary gap.* Abingdon, UK: Routledge.

Rasinski, T. V. (2006). Reading fluency instruction: Moving beyond accuracy, automaticity, and prosody. *The Reading Teacher, 59,* 704–706.

Rasinski, T. V., & Cheesman Smith, M. (2018). *The megabook of fluency.* New York, NY: Scholastic.

Rasinski, T. V., & Padak, N. (2005). *Three-minute reading assessments: Word recognition, fluency, and comprehension for grades 1–4.* New York, NY: Scholastic.

Rasinski, T. V., Rikli, A., & Johnston, S. (2009). Reading fluency: More than automaticity? More than a concern for the primary grades? *Literacy Research and Instruction, 48*(4), 350–361. doi:10.1080/19388070802468715.

Rastle, K. (2019). EPS mid-career prize lecture: Writing systems, reading and language. *Quarterly Journal of Experimental Psychology, 72*(4), 677–692. https://doi.org/10.1177/1747021819829696.

Rayner, K., & Duffy, A. (1986). Lexical complexity and fixation times in reading: Effects of word frequency, verb complexity, and lexical ambiguity. *Memory and Cognition, 14,* 191–201.

Reading Rockets (2019). List-group-label. Retrieved from www.readingrockets.org/strategies/list_group_label.

Reed, D. K., Petscher, V., & Truckenmiller, A. J. (2016). The contribution of general reading ability to science achievement. *Reading Research Quarterly, 52*(2), 253–266.

Resnick, L., Asterhan, C., & Clarke, S. (2018). *Accountable talk: Instructional dialogue that builds the mind. educational practices series.* International Academy of Education and the International

Bureau of Education. Retrieved from www.researchgate.net/publication/324830361_Accountable_Talk_Instructional_dialogue_that_builds_the_mind.

Reynolds, T., & Rush, L. S. (2017). Experts and novices reading literature: An analysis of disciplinary literacy in English language arts. *Literacy Research and Instruction, 56*(3), 199–216. doi:10.1080/19388071.2017.1299820.

Rinehart, S. D., Stahl, S. A., & Erickson, L. G. (1986). Some effects of summarization training on reading and studying. *Reading Research Quarterly, 21*, 422–438.

Roberts, J., Winter, K., & Connolly, P. (2017). The Letterbox Club book gifting intervention: Findings from a qualitative evaluation accompanying a randomised trial. *Children and Youth Services Review, 73*, 467–473.

Robinson, L., & Merrell, C. (2017). *Improving reading: A guide for teachers.* Durham, UK: Centre for Evaluation and Monitoring, Durham University. Retrieved from https://bit.ly/2l3iseN.

Rodd, J. (2017). Lexical ambiguity. In M. G. Gaskell & S. A. Rueschemeyer (Eds.), *Oxford handbook of psycholinguistics.* Oxford: Oxford University Press. Retrieved from https://psyarxiv.com/yezc6.

Roehling, J. V., Hebert, M., Nelson, J. R. R., & Bohaty, J. J. (2017). Text structure strategies for improving expository reading comprehension. *The Reading Teacher, 71*(1), 71–82. doi:10.1002/trtr.1590.

Rose, J. (2006). *Independent review of the teaching of early reading.* London: DfE.

Rose, J. (2009). *Identifying and teaching children and young people with dyslexia and literacy difficulties.* An independent report from Sir Jim Rose to the Secretary of State for Children, Schools and Families. Retrieved from http://webarchive.nationalarchives.gov.uk/20130401151715/www.education.gov.uk/   publications/eorderingdownload/00659-2009dom-en.pdf.

Rosenblatt, L. M. (1960). Literature: The reader's role. *English Journal, 49*(5), 304–310, 315–316. http://links.jstor.org/sici?sici=00138274%28196005%2949%3A5%3C304%3ALTRR%3E2.0.CO%3B2-3.

Rowling, J. K. (1997). *Harry Potter and the philosopher's stone.* London: Bloomsbury.

Rundell, K. (2019). Words for life interview. Retrieved from www.wordsforlife.org.uk/katherine-rundell.

Ryan, L. (Ed.) (2016). *AQA GCSE chemistry.* Oxford: Oxford University Press.

Saenger, P. (1997). *Space between words: The origins of silent reading.* Stanford, CA: Stanford University Press.

Bibliography

Samuels, S. J., & Farstrup, A. E. (2011). *What the research has to say about reading instruction* (4th ed.). Newark, DE: International Reading Association.

Save the Children (2014). *Read on, get on: How reading can help children escape poverty.* London: Save the Children.

Scanlon, D. M., Anderson, K. L., & Sweeney, J. M. (2017). *Early intervention for reading difficulties: The interactive strategies approach* (2nd ed.). London: Guilford Press.

Scarborough, H. S. (2001). Connecting early language and literacy to later reading (dis)abilities: Evidence, theory, and practice. In S. Neuman & D. Dickinson (Eds.), *Handbook for research in early literacy* (pp. 97–110) . New York, NY: Guilford Press.

Schell, V. (1982). Learning partners: Reading and mathematics. *The Reading Teacher, 35*(5), 544–548.

Schleppegrell, M. J. (2007). The linguistic challenges of mathematics teaching and learning: A research review. *Reading & Writing Quarterly, 23*(2), 139–159.

Schultz, P. (2011). *My dyslexia.* New York, NY: W. W. Norton & Company.

Schwidt-Wiegard, F., Kohnert, A., & Glowalla, U. (2010). A closer look at split visual attention in system- and self-paced instruction in multimedia learning. *Learning and Instruction, 20*(2), 100–110.

Sedita, J. (2005). Effective vocabulary instruction. *Insights on Learning Disabilities, 2*(1), 33–45.

Seidenberg, M. (2013). The science of reading and its educational implications. *Language Learning and Development, 9*(4), 331–360. doi:10.1080/15475441.2013.812017.

Seidenberg, M. (2017). *Reading at the speed of sight: Why we read, why so many can't and what we can do about it.* New York, NY: Basic Books.

Shanahan, C. (2015). *Disciplinary literacy strategies in content area classes.* Newark, DE: International Literacy Association.

Shanahan, C., Bolz, M. J., Cribb, G., Goldman, S. R., Heppeler, J., & Manderino, M. (2016). Deepening what it means to read (and write) like a historian: Progressions of instruction across a school year in an eleventh grade U.S. history class. *The History Teacher, 49*(2), 241–270.

Shanahan, C., & Shanahan, T. (2014). The implications of disciplinary literacy. *Journal of Adolescent and Adult Literacy, 57*(8), 628–631.

Shanahan, T. (2017). What is close reading? Retrieved from https://shanahanonliteracy.com/blog/what-is-close-reading.

Shanahan, T. (2018). Which is best? Analytic or synthetic phonics? Retrieved from www.readingrockets.org/blogs/shanahan-literacy/which-best-analytic-or-synthetic-phonics.

Shanahan, T. (2019). Is round-robin reading really that bad? Retrieved from www.shanahanonliteracy.com/blog/is-round-robin-reading-really-that-bad.

Shanahan, T., & Shanahan, C. (2008). Teaching disciplinary literacy to adolescents: Rethinking content-area literacy. *Harvard Educational Review, 78*(1), 40–59.

Shanahan, T., & Shanahan, C. (2012). What is disciplinary literacy and why does it matter? *Topics in Language Disorders, 32*(1), 7–18. doi:10.1097/TLD.0b013e318244557a.

Shanahan, T., & Shanahan, C. (2017). Disciplinary literacy: Just the FAQs. *Educational Leadership: Journal of the Department of Supervision and Curriculum Development, N.E.A., 74*(5), 18–22.

Shaywitz, S. E. (1996). Dyslexia. *Scientific American*, November, 98–104.

Shulman, L. (2004). *The wisdom of practice: Collected essays of Lee Shulman: Volume 1.* San Francisco, CA: Jossey-Bass.

Siebert, D., & Draper, R. J. (2008). Why content-area literacy messages do not speak to mathematics teachers: A critical content analysis. *Literacy Research and Instruction, 47*(4), 229–245. doi:10.1080/19388070802300314.

Snow, C. E. (2002). *Reading for understanding: Toward a research and development programme in reading comprehension.* London: Rand Corporation.

Snow, C. E., & Juel, C. (2005). Teaching children to read: What do we know about how to do it? In M. J. Snowling & C. Hulme (Eds.), *The science of reading: A handbook* (pp. 501–520). Malden, MA: Blackwell.

Snowling, M. J. (2008). Specific disorders and broader phenotypes: The case of dyslexia. *Quarterly Journal of Experimental Psychology, 61*(1), 142–156. https://doi.org/10.1080/17470210701508830.

Snowling, M. J. (2014). Dyslexia: A language learning impairment. *Journal of the British Academy, 2*, 43–58.

Snowling, M. J. (2018). Language: The elephant in the reading room. Retrieved from https://readoxford.org/language-the-elephant-in-the-reading-room.

Snowling, M., Hulme, C., Bailey, A., Stothard, S., & Lindsay, G. (2011). *Better communication research programme: Language and literacy attainment of pupils during early years and through KS2: Does teacher assessment at five provide a valid measure of children's current and future educational attainments?* Department for Education Research Report, 172a. London: Department for Education.

Spencer, M., Wagner, R. K., & Petscher, Y. (2019). The reading comprehension and vocabulary knowledge of children with poor reading comprehension despite adequate decoding: Evidence from

Bibliography

a regression-based matching approach. *Journal of Educational Psychology, 111*(1), 1–14. http://dx.doi.org/10.1037/edu0000274.

Stahl, S. A. (1999). *Vocabulary development.* Cambridge, MA: Brookline Books.

Stanovich, K. E. (1986). Matthew effects in reading: Some consequences of individual differences in the acquisition of literacy. *Reading Research Quarterly, 21,* 360–407.

Stockwell, F. (2007). *A history of information storage and retrieval.* Jefferson, NC: McFarland & Co.

Stoddard, K., Valcante, G., Sindelar, P., O'Shea, L., & Algozzin, B. (1993). Increasing reading rate and comprehension: The effects of repeated readings, sentence segmentation, and intonation training. *Literacy Research and Instruction, 32*(4), 53–65. doi:10.1080/19388079309558133.

Sullivan, A., & Brown, M. (2013). *Social inequalities in cognitive scores at age 16: The role of reading.* London: Centre of Longitudinal Studies.

Sullivan, A., Moulton, V., & Fitzsimons, E. (2017). *The intergenerational transmission of vocabulary.* Working paper 2017/14. London: UCL.

Suttle, C. M., Lawrenson, J. G., & Conway, M. L. (2018). Efficacy of coloured overlays and lenses for treating reading difficulty: An overview of systematic reviews. *Clinical and Experimental Optometry, 101*(4), 514–520.

Taboada, A., Tonks, S., Wigfield, A., & Guthrie, J. T. (2009). Effects of motivational and cognitive variables on reading comprehension. *Reading & Writing Quarterly, 22,* 85–106.

Teacher Tapp (2018). What teacher tapped this week. No. 60, 19 November. Retrieved from https://teachertapp.co.uk/what-teacher-tapped-this-week-60-19th-november-2018.

Tennant, W. (2014). *Understanding reading comprehension: Processes and practices.* London: Sage.

Tenner , E. (2006). Searching for dummies. *New York Times.* Retrieved from www.nytimes.com/2006/03/26/opinion/searching-for-dummies.html.

Texas Education Agency (n.d.). Fluency: Instructional guidelines and student activities. Retrieved from www.readingrockets.org/article/fluency-instructional-guidelines-and-student-activities.

Therrien, W. J., & Kubina, R. M., Jr (2006). Developing reading fluency with repeated reading. *Intervention in School and Clinic, 41*(3), 156–160.

Thompson, D. R., & Rubenstein, R. N. (2000). Learning mathematics vocabulary: Potential pitfalls and instructional strategies. *The Mathematics Teacher, 93*(7), 568–574.

Treiman, R. (2018). What research tells us about reading instruction. *Psychological Science in the Public Interest, 19*(1), 1–4.

van Bergen, E., Snowling, M. J., de Zeeuw, E. L., van Beijsterveldt, C. E. M., Dolan, C. V., & Boomsma, D. I. (2018). Why do children read more? The influence of reading ability on voluntary reading practices. *Journal of Child Psychology and Psychiatry, 59*(11), 1205–1214.

van der Schoot, M., Reijntjes, A., & van Lieshout, E. C. D. M. (2012). How do children deal with inconsistencies in text? An eye fixation and self-paced reading study in good and poor reading comprehenders. *Reading and Writing, 25*(7), 1665–1690. doi:10.1007/s11145-011-9337-4.

Vellutino, F. R., Fletcher, J. M., Snowling, M. J., & Scanlon, D. M. (2004). Specific reading disability (dyslexia): What have we learned from the past four decades? *Journal of Child Psychology Psychiatry, 45*(1), 2–40.

Walsh, D. J., Price, G. G., & Gillingham, M. G. (1988). The critical but transitory importance of letter naming. *Reading Research Quarterly, 23*,108–122.

Warren, T., White, S. J., & Reichie, E. D. (2005). Investigating the causes of wrap-up effects: Evidence from eye movements and E–Z reader. *Cognition, 111*, 132–137.

Westbrook, J., Sutherland, J., Oakhill, J. V., & Sullivan, S. (2018). 'Just reading': The impact of a faster pace of reading narratives on the comprehension of poorer adolescent readers in English classrooms. *Literacy, 53*(2), 60–68.

Wexler, J., Mitchell, M. A., Clancy, E. E., & Silverman, R. D. (2017). An investigation of literacy practices in high school science classrooms. *Reading and Writing Quarterly, 33*(3), 258–277. http://dx.doi.org/10.1080/10573569.2016.1193832.

Wexler, N. (2019). *The knowledge gap: The hidden cause of America's broken education system – and how to fix it.* New York, NY: Avery.

What Works Clearinghouse (2016). *Foundational skills to support reading for understanding in kindergarten through 3rd grade.* Washington, DC: Institution of Education Sciences (IES), US Department of Education.

Wigfield, A., & Guthrie, J. T. (1997). Relations of children's motivation for reading to the amount and breadth of their reading. *Journal of Educational Psychology, 89*, 420–432.

Wilkerson, I., Murphy, K., & Binici, S. (2015). Dialogue-intensive pedagogies for promoting reading comprehension: What we know, what we need to know. In L. Resnick, C. Asterhan, & S. Clarke (Eds.), *Socializing intelligence through academic talk and dialogue* (pp. 37–50). Washington, DC: American Educational Research Association.

Bibliography

Willingham, D. (2006). How knowledge helps. *American Educator.* Retrieved from www.aft.org/periodical/american-educator/spring-2006/how-knowledge-helps.

Willingham, D. (2015). *Raising kids who read: What parents and teachers can do.* San Francisco, CA: Jossey-Bass.

Willingham, D. (2017). *The reading mind: A cognitive approach to understanding how the mind reads.* San Francisco, CA: Jossey-Bass.

Wineburg, S. S. (1991). Historical problem solving: A study of the cognitive processes used in the evaluation of documentary and pictorial evidence. *Journal of Educational Psychology, 83*(1), 73–87. doi:10.1037/0022-0663.83.1.73.

Woelfle, G., *Katje the windmill cat.* London: Walker Books.

Woolf, M. (2008). *Proust and the squid: The story and science of the reading brain.* Cambridge, UK: Icon Books.

Woolf, M. (2009). *Reader come home: The reading brain in a digital world.* New York, NY: Harper Collins.

Woolf, V. (1927). *To the lighthouse.* Oxford: Oxford University Press.

Woolf, V. (2015). *The moment and other essays.* A Project Gutenberg e-book Retrieved from www.gutenberg.net.au/ebooks15/1500221h.html.

Woore, R., Graham, S., Porter, A., Courtney, L., & Savory, C. (2018). *Foreign language education unlocking reading (FLEUR): A study into the teaching of reading to beginner learners of French in secondary school.* Retrieved from https://bit.ly/2Qc7Mcg.

Vaknin-Nusbaum, V., Nevo, E., Brande, S., & Gambrell, L. (2018). Developmental aspects of reading motivation and reading achievement among second grade lo achievers and typical readers. *Journal of Research in Reading, 41*(3), 438–454.

Young, N. D. (2017). *From floundering to fluent: Reading and teaching struggling readers.* London: Rowman & Littlefield.

Zutell, J., & Rasinski, T. V. (1991). Training teachers to attend to their students' oral reading fluency. *Theory to Practice, 30,* 211–217.

Index

Index

Index

Index